Here's What Others Are Saying About
Creating Personal Presence

"My kind of book! Either saddle up and ride or go sit in the truck! Dianna is the expert on becoming a winning presence!"
—**Jeffrey Hayzlett, business cowboy; former Chief Marketing Officer, Kodak; and author of *The Mirror Test***

"Great ideas are of no value if they cannot be effectively communicated to others. It has everything to do with personal presence."
—**Ralph D. Heath, Executive Vice President, Lockheed Martin Aeronautics Company**

"This is a gem of a book. Not only has Booher made the intangible concept of presence accessible, she has done so in an entertaining, compelling manner. This book should be mandatory reading for all current and future leaders."
—**Robba Benjamin, former Vice President and General Manager, Consumer Line of Business, Cisco Systems, Inc.**

"Highly recommended for anyone who wants to increase his or her impact as a leader."
—**Daniel Burrus, author of the New York Times bestseller *Flash Foresight***

"The perfect resource from Dianna Booher—the gold standard in communications coaching. I'll order hundreds of copies for our leaders."
—**Jane Binger, EdD, Executive Director, Leadership Development and Education, Lucile Packard Children's Hospital, Stanford University**

"For the star performer just starting out or the seasoned pro, this book provides hundreds of practical tips to build credibility and expand influence."
—**Mira Marr, Vice President, Corporate University, Army & Air Force Exchange Service**

"What an extraordinary work in a most substantive area. I recommend this book unreservedly."

—Dr. Nido R. Qubein, President, High Point University, and Chairman, Great Harvest Bread Company

"Practical tips. Well researched. Entertaining anecdotes. Helpful checklists. A big winner."

—Dr. Tony Alessandra, coauthor of *The New Art of Managing People and The Platinum Rule*

CREATING
PERSONAL
PRESENCE

Other Books by Dianna Booher

. . . .

Communicate with Confidence! How to Say It Right the First Time and Every Time

Speak with Confidence: Powerful Presentations That Inform, Inspire, and Persuade

The Voice of Authority: 10 Communication Strategies Every Leader Needs to Know

Booher's Rules of Business Grammar: 101 Fast and Easy Ways to Correct the Most Common Errors

Good Grief, Good Grammar: The Businessperson's Guide to Grammar and Usage

E-Writing: 21st-Century Tools for Effective Communication

From Contact to Contract

Your Signature Work

Your Signature Life

Great Personal Letters for Busy People: 501 Ready-to-Use Letters for Every Occasion

10 Smart Moves for Women Who Want to Succeed in Love and Life

Executive's Portfolio of Model Speeches for All Occasions

Get a Life Without Sacrificing Your Career: How to Find Time for What's Really Important

Get Ahead! Stay Ahead! Learn the 70 Most Important Career Skills, Traits and Attitudes to Stay Employed! Get Promoted! Get a Better Job!

The Little Book of Big Questions

Love Notes: From My Heart to Yours

Fresh-Cut Flowers for a Friend

The Worth of a Woman's Words

CREATING PERSONAL PRESENCE

Look, Talk, Think, and Act Like a Leader

· ·

Dianna Booher

· ·

BK

Berrett–Koehler Publishers, Inc.
San Francisco
a BK Life book

Berrett-Koehler Publishers, Inc.
235 Montgomery Street, Suite 650, San Francisco, CA 94104-2916
Tel: (415) 288-0260   Fax: (415) 362-2512   www.bkconnection.com

Ordering Information
Quantity sales. Special discounts are available on quantity purchases by corporations, associations, and others. For details, contact the "Special Sales Department" at the Berrett-Koehler address above.
Individual sales. Berrett-Koehler publications are available through most bookstores. They can also be ordered directly from Berrett-Koehler: Tel: (800) 929-2929; Fax: (802) 864-7626; www.bkconnection.com
Orders for college textbook/course adoption use. Please contact Berrett-Koehler: Tel: (800) 929-2929; Fax: (802) 864-7626.
Orders by U.S. trade bookstores and wholesalers. Please contact Ingram Publisher Services, Tel: (800) 509-4887; Fax: (800) 838-1149; E-mail: customer.service@ingram publisherservices.com; or visit www.ingrampublisherservices.com/Ordering for details about electronic ordering.

Berrett-Koehler and the BK logo are registered trademarks of Berrett-Koehler Publishers, Inc.

Printed in the United States of America

Berrett-Koehler books are printed on long-lasting acid-free paper. When it is available, we choose paper that has been manufactured by environmentally responsible processes. These may include using trees grown in sustainable forests, incorporating recycled paper, minimizing chlorine in bleaching, or recycling the energy produced at the paper mill.

LIBRARY OF CONGRESS CATALOGING-IN-PUBLICATION DATA
Booher, Dianna Daniels.
Creating personal presence : look, talk, think, and act like a leader / Dianna Booher.
—1st ed.
p. cm.
Includes bibliographical references and index.
ISBN 978-1-60994-011-9 (pbk. : alk. paper)
1. Leadership—Psychological aspects. 2. Self-confidence. I. Title.
HD57.7.B6566 2011
658.4'092--dc23
2011027384
First Edition
16 15 14 13 12 11   10 9 8 7 6 5 4 3 2 1

Cover design: Barbara Haines
Produced by Wilsted & Taylor Publishing Services
Copyediting: Jennifer Brown   Design: Jody Hanson   Indexing: Andrew Joron

To my parents,
Alton and Opal Daniels,
for their loving support
in everything I undertake

Contents

Preface

About fifteen years ago, in the middle of a keynote address before approximately 3,500 people, I asked for two volunteers to join me on stage to demonstrate the principles of presence. I'd never tried the experiment before in front of such a large group, and frankly, I was a little nervous. What if nobody volunteered? What if the volunteers were so timid that I couldn't help them? What if they were already so strong that I couldn't think of any coaching tips to increase their impact?

The first volunteer steps up on the stage, takes the handheld microphone, introduces herself, and overviews a key project she's working on. After thirty seconds, I call out, "Stop!" Then I pull her aside privately for sixty seconds and give her a couple of coaching tips. She returns to center stage and repeats her introduction.

After the "before" and "after" demonstration, I ask people in the audience to go to the microphones in the aisles and call out the difference in the speaker's impact. They call out adjectives I expect, "More confident." "More engaging." "More commanding." "More authoritative. More credible." All adjectives I expect, so I'm pleased. Yet I had used none of those words in coaching her.

"Did I tell you to be or do any of that?" I ask the volunteer.

"No," she chuckles, obviously pleased with her performance and feedback.

I ask for a second volunteer. Four or five people raise their hands, and I again select someone to join me on stage. As soon as he starts down the aisle toward me, I panic. His gait is halting, and he looks very stiff. Uh-ooooh, I'm in trouble. When he takes the microphone, his voice sounds like a twelve-year-old. Again, thirty seconds into it, I yell, "Stop." Same routine—sixty seconds of coaching tips.

He does version two. The crowd goes wild with applause and whistling. It's like he turns into a rock star. He keeps performing. "Plant." "Plant!" "He's a plant!"

It took me a couple of seconds to figure out what several audience members were chanting. The change was so miraculous that they thought I had planted that volunteer in the group and that he was playacting his transformation. When I finally got the handheld mic back from him, both he and I assured the crowd that this was the first time we'd met. We finished the experiment, and I thanked both volunteers and wrapped up my program.

Afterward, the volunteers waited until the crowd around the stage dispersed, and then they thanked me again. Both volunteers reported to me that several people from the audience had come up to them after the program to ask privately once again for their assurance that they were not "plants" and that the changes they'd made on stage were really just a result of doing only two or three physical things that I'd coached them to do in the sixty-second conference on stage.

The response to that demonstration was so dramatic that I began to include it in every talk I made on the topic of presence and personal credibility. It soon became my most requested speaking topic. Calls to our office typically started with, "I was in an audience where Dianna had volunteers come up on stage . . ."

But despite that positive reaction to the speech and even though I've written many books touching other aspects of communication, I continued to nix the idea of a book on this topic because I considered "presence" something that you have to see rather than just read about. Yet, in the intervening years since that first onstage demonstration, question after question has come up from coaching clients that has led me to decide differently.

Maybe I can, after all, put the essence of presence on a page. This book is that effort, and you can decide if I've been successful.

If you've picked up this book, you probably fit my definition of a leader or an aspiring leader. Leaders never limit themselves by titles. You'll find them in all walks of life: CEOs and sales professionals, first-level supervisors and department heads, volunteers serving nonprofits, soldiers serving their country, homeowners organizing their communities, parents coaching youth teams. Anyone with a mission becomes a leader by persuading others to follow in achieving an important goal.

The book's purpose is to make the concept of personal presence concrete and thereby "doable." Of course, you can never measure presence in the same sense that you can measure, say, someone's heart rate or their running speed.

But consider for a moment how we measure a singer's ability. The long-running popular TV show *American Idol* comes to mind. Who's the best singer-performer of the season? Granted, these ratings are based on subjective opinions of the judges and the viewers—to a degree. But there are concrete assessments involved at some point as well. Contestants have to demonstrate some level of competence or they get booted off the show—many before the season even starts. They either can or can't sing on key. They have a definite vocal range—one that the judges assess to be adequate or inadequate for the competition. They can or can't keep a beat. Then beyond the baseline of those competencies in music, subjectivity comes into play.

The same holds true for presence. This book aims to capture these core concepts about presence. Beyond these, what you see and hear comes down to others' perception of our presence. The book will also delve into the subjective realm—what affects others subjective perceptions about your presence and credibility.

The book falls easily into four parts:

"Part 1: How You Look" contains five chapters having to do with the physical aspects of presence: appearance, body language, dress, walk, your surroundings.

"Part 2: How You Talk" includes five chapters on voice quality, word choices, and your ability to carry on engaging and meaningful conversations.

"Part 3: How You Think" covers how you process your

thoughts and information and express those thoughts to others: your ability to sort the significant from the trivial, to summarize succinctly, and to respond to questions under pressure. This section also addresses the difference between strategic thinking and tactical thinking. Finally, you'll find a chapter on controlling your reactions and expressing emotions appropriately.

"Part 4: How to Act" deals with attitude and character traits that come across in your communication style—attitudes, habits, and behaviors that either support or diminish a powerful presence and your resulting credibility.

As I mentioned earlier, the goal is to help you increase your presence, so I've tried to be as specific as possible with tips, techniques, and anecdotes to make the principles understandable and practical. Please note, however, that although the anecdotes are factual, I've changed the names in each to protect identities.

If you're reading this book, chances are you already understand the power of presence to:

- Persuade others as you state opinions and answer questions.
- Position yourself as a thought leader when you champion a cause or a change.
- Communicate issues clearly in ways that engage others both intellectually and emotionally.
- Win others' trust by demonstrating your integrity and goodwill.
- Win contracts or promotions and generally get ahead in your career.

But your organization will benefit as well. The stronger your presence as their spokesperson, the better your chances to represent them well, to champion their cause, sell their product or service, generate goodwill, demonstrate integrity and win trust for their purposes.

To further increase your awareness of your own presence, I've created The Personal Presence Self-Assessment (available from

Berrett-Koehler Publishers at www.bkconnection.com/personal presence-sa) to help you assess yourself in four key areas covered in the book. Take the self-assessment either before you read the book to guide you on where to focus first in the book or afterward when you're putting together your individual and organizational action plan.

As I wrap up here, I want to thank the team at Berrett-Koehler for all their efforts along the way in shepherding this book from idea to bookshelf to you. Specifically, appreciation goes to Steve Piersanti, editor-in-chief, who "got it" right from the beginning and understood how this book could be different from the bazillion others on communication, presentation skills, and interpersonal skills. Thanks also to David Marshall, Kristen Frantz, Marina Cook, Michael Crowley, Zoe Mackey, Katie Sheehan, Cynthia Shannon, Johanna Vondeling, Maria Aguilo, Catherine Lengronne, Dianne Platner, Rick Wilson, Bonnie Kaufman, Jeevan Sivasubramanian, and Neal Maillet.

Also, once again thanks to our Booher team of consultants who generate rave reviews in the marketplace. They continually accept new client challenges, develop strategies, and deliver results that help us fine-tune best practices in the many facets of personal and organizational communication.

Special thanks as well to Kari Gates and Polly Fuhrman for assistance with research and manuscript preparation.

Finally, my gratitude goes to literally thousands of you as clients who have provided us the opportunity to work with you on the strategies in this book, hear your feedback, see the results, and feel the satisfaction of your success. A heartfelt thanks!

—*Dianna Booher*

Why Should You Care?

Lydia (not her real name) told a different story from what I'd heard from the senior partner in her Washington D.C. law firm. "I feel as though I'm pushing against that proverbial glass ceiling," she said. "I just don't get the plum assignments. I put in the hours. On performance reviews, my director has given me the highest marks for attitude, legal competence, that sort of thing. But I'm just not getting the opportunities to network and deal with clients to bring in the business. Sure, I'm on the 'team,' but I'm never the *lead* counsel. That's what you have to do to make partner—bring in the business. And if I don't make partner in the next year or two, I'm out."

She paused reflectively before concluding, "Most all the partners in the firm are male. Whether intentional or not, I really think there's a bias there that's keeping me from getting in front of clients. It just has to be the gender thing."

It was not the gender thing.

The senior partner of the law firm had called a week earlier with his feedback on Lydia and his goals for our coaching session together. The upshot of his call was this: "Lydia's very competent legally. And she's very willing to put in the hours. But to date, we've been hesitant to put her in front of our clients or in the courtroom. I can't put my finger on what it is exactly, but she just lacks presence and polish. That's what I'm hoping you can accomplish with her."

He proceeded to describe several symptoms, including this particular comment that stands out in my memory: "Even the way she introduces herself when she and the team meet clients or prospects for the first time minimizes her experience and our expertise as a firm. I've tried to give her a few pointers myself, but she doesn't take feedback well."

Although dressed in a business suit as typical for her profession, Lydia arrived looking at least a decade out of step. In addition to the cold-fish handshake, her energy level seemed no higher than thirty watts. Her voice, too, lacked intensity. A permanent furrow seemed etched across her forehead. As I introduced her to others on my staff, she had difficulty chatting with them as they gathered for morning coffee. When I asked about interactions with clients and other executives in the firm, she rambled and lacked a strategic focus about the organization's goals. To most of my suggestions, her responses were "yes, but . . ." followed by a justification.

The first few minutes into our coaching session, I arrived at the same conclusion as her boss: Lydia lacked presence, and unfortunately for her future with the firm, she didn't take feedback well. Typically when clients leave a coaching session, they comment on how they plan to put the new skills and ideas into practice and promise to call back with the results.

I never heard from Lydia again.

On the other hand, Jon, CEO of a major aerospace defense contractor, profited handsomely from feedback. At the end of one of our coaching sessions, Jon said to me, "Okay, so tell me how to dress. I'm an engineer and I don't usually pay attention to that sort of thing. I'm divorced. Don't have a wife to give me opinions anymore. But I know it's important. And Kathryn, our VP of

Communications, told me I need to get your opinion on dress for my first all-hands meeting and my speech for the conference in Germany. Colors? Button jacket or leave it open?"

We worked on his opening, a personal anecdote, for the all-hands speech for almost two hours, because his goal was to set the tone for the new direction for the company and inspire confidence in his ability to chart that new course.

Seemingly small things can make a big impact.

The "little" things can make a big difference in landing a job, getting a promotion, winning a contract, or leading an organization through change—as Jon, the new CEO, understood in successfully leading his organization to regain its position as industry leader. He won the hearts and minds of his organization with his first "state of the organization" speech to employees after assuming his office.

For the next six months as I was in and out of the organization, other executives commented on Jon as if he'd become a celebrity after his debut address. He had developed presence, and it had a huge impact—on him and his organization.

Personal presence may be difficult to define, but we all know it when we see it. Someone walks into the room and people step aside. Heads turn. Conversation opens up to include them. When they speak, people applaud or chime in. When they ask, people answer. When they lead, people follow. When they leave, things wind down.

People with presence look confident and comfortable, speak clearly and persuasively, think clearly even under pressure. They act with intention. People with presence reflect on their emotions, attitudes, and situations and then adapt. They accept responsibility for themselves and the results they achieve. People with presence are real. They present their genuine character authentically. What they say and do matches who they are.

Mother Teresa was as welcome and comfortable in the world's boardrooms as the most articulate CEO, the best-dressed movie star, or high-earning sports celebrity. At just five feet tall, dressed in her traditional habit, with few earthly possessions to call her own, Mother Teresa had at least one secret that many imitators lack. And unfortunately, this one—or its absence—takes a while to surface: character.

For forty-five years, armed with little but her integrity, her tongue, and her ability to make CEOs feel the plight of the poor, Mother Teresa persuaded them to finance her goals: orphanages, hospices, leper houses, hospitals, and soup kitchens. By the time of her death, 123 countries on six continents had felt her personal presence.

Presence can help you get a date, a mate, or a sale. Presence can help you lead a meeting, a movement, a revolution, or a nation. Presence appears in all segments of society and all levels of an organization.

Presence may be used for noble purposes or selfish goals. When politicians, athletes, movie stars, or managers slip into crass or manipulative behavior, we boycott their events, bad-mouth their leadership, and say they have no class.

Wherever you are and wherever you want to go, presence can help you get there.

I'm convinced that Mother Teresa had studied Aristotle. Back in the fourth century, he identified three essentials of persuasive communication—another big component of personal presence:

— logical argument (the ability to articulate your points clearly)
— emotion (the ability to create or control emotion in your listeners)
— character (the ability to convey integrity and goodwill)

Times haven't changed all that much. Being a skilled communicator—a huge part of personal presence—still grants social status and influence. In fact, communication makes leadership possible—in politics, in the community, in the workplace, in the family. Think how often pundits and voters alike point out a candidate's speaking ability and social skills—or lack thereof. Not only do we expect our presidents and celebrities to speak well, but also that has become the expected norm for CEOs, system analysts, sales professionals, and soccer moms.

As I mentioned in the Preface, you can never measure presence in the same sense that you can measure someone's heart rate or their running speed. Measuring someone's presence falls more along the lines of measuring their health. Generally, physicians can check reflexes, do an EKG, give a stress test, check cholesterol levels, do a blood and urine analysis, give a vision and hearing exam, and then certify that someone is free of disease and physically fit or unfit. Beyond that baseline of health, subjectivity comes into play. Individuals compete among themselves and against their own personal standards for healthy living according to the energy levels they want and lifestyles they want to lead.

But there are substantive core concepts involved at some point as well as subjectivity.

The same holds true for personal presence. This book aims to capture these core concepts about presence. Beyond these, what you see and hear comes down to others' perception of your presence. The book will also delve into the subjective realm—what affects others' subjective perceptions about your presence and credibility.

At work, the limiting label generally comes down to some supervisor's statement on a performance appraisal or around a conference room table that the person under discussion lacks "polish."

Often we hear entire groups of rising superstars in an organization categorized and set aside for special mentoring or training this way: "These are the high potentials. We've identified them early on for key projects and high-visibility assignments in front of the executive team. We need you to help them add the finishing touches."

Although they are technically competent, someone at the top has decided that they need more presence to make the next career jump. Certain commonalities always surface—common traits and attitudes among the candidates, as well as similar remarks from the executives sending them for the coaching.

— "Brilliant. But not well liked. Just doesn't connect with people."
— "Doesn't always use the appropriate language—too flippant, too laid back."

— "Too stiff, always looks a little nervous, with that deer-in-the-headlights look."
— "Comes on too strong. Needs to dial it back."
— "Doesn't dress appropriately. Just not what I call classy."
— "Rambles. Knows her stuff, but gets off track and down in the weeds too easily."
— "Tentative. Needs confidence."
— "Too intense."
— "Has difficulty facilitating a meeting with a lot of strong personalities in the room."

Whatever the comment, the superstar has hit a wall for a reason, and he or she has no idea what it is or how to "fix it." Most people are aware, however, of the advantages increased presence brings them. They understand that influence demands personal presence.

This special categorization of "high potential" and help has been offered, not because this group of individuals ranks low on the continuum of personal presence. Exactly the opposite. They get tagged for "polish" because they already rank high on that continuum of presence and have shown excellent skills, potential, commitment, and interest in increasing their influence and impact to an even greater degree in the organization.

Presence is not an all-or-nothing commodity. Consider a continuum or a funnel such as you see in the chart below, with your physical attributes, natural talents, communication skills, and character traits plotted along the way somewhere from one end to the other between "low presence/low impact" and "high presence/high impact." All of us can inch a little closer to the high end every day as we present ourselves with awareness and intention.

Booher Consultants surveyed more than two hundred professionals across multiple industries to ask respondents their reasons for wanting to increase their personal presence. Forty-eight percent responded that their reason was either to "increase credibility in the organization" or "sell my ideas and projects." Our consultants have been hearing the same reasons for the past thirty years as they've coached individual clients.

Our survey asked this question: "In general, how much does someone's personal presence affect how much credibility they have with you?" "A great deal" was the response from 74.5 percent of the survey participants.

So how do you make sure that you develop that certain mystique of personal presence?

Understand that there really is no mystery after all. This book picks up the baton where Aristotle left it: Becoming a persuasive communicator leads to credibility and influence. And you can develop those skills and attributes. You can have the same effect as CEOs, celebrities, civic leaders, and any influential individual if you develop your personal presence to its greatest impact.

The following chapters will provide practical tips and techniques that will help you connect with others and communicate with credibility, power, and significance. You've heard it said that someone has "the presence of mind" to do X. Likewise, this book covers the mental, physical, and emotional aspects of presence. To put it simply, your personal presence involves how you:

— **look** (your body language, handshake, movement, dress, surroundings)
— **talk** (the words you choose, the physical qualities of your voice, how you use your voice)
— **think** and communicate your thoughts (how you organize ideas and information, what you decide to pass on or withhold, how you frame issues)
— **act** (the attitudes, values, and competence your actions reveal)

As you increase your personal presence, you will strengthen your credibility and expand your influence. With that stronger impact, you'll increase your chances of achieving your personal and career goals and the mission and goals of your organization.

PERSONAL PRESENCE

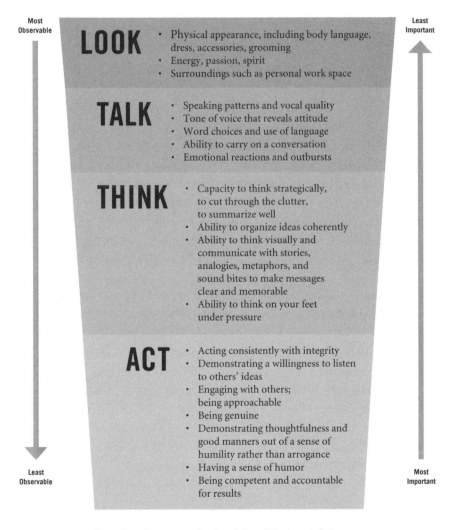

Most
Observable

Least
Important

LOOK
- Physical appearance, including body language, dress, accessories, grooming
- Energy, passion, spirit
- Surroundings such as personal work space

TALK
- Speaking patterns and vocal quality
- Tone of voice that reveals attitude
- Word choices and use of language
- Ability to carry on a conversation
- Emotional reactions and outbursts

THINK
- Capacity to think strategically, to cut through the clutter, to summarize well
- Ability to organize ideas coherently
- Ability to think visually and communicate with stories, analogies, metaphors, and sound bites to make messages clear and memorable
- Ability to think on your feet under pressure

ACT
- Acting consistently with integrity
- Demonstrating a willingness to listen to others' ideas
- Engaging with others; being approachable
- Being genuine
- Demonstrating thoughtfulness and good manners out of a sense of humility rather than arrogance
- Having a sense of humor
- Being competent and accountable for results

Least
Observable

Most
Important

Your character serves as the foundation of the funnel. But your appearance is typically what others observe first about you. As you develop your presence in all four areas, you will increase your impact.

Specifically, you'll learn to:

- Think on your feet under pressure as you state opinions and answer questions.
- Cut through the clutter and communicate issues clearly in ways that engage others both intellectually and emotionally.
- Win others' trust by identifying specific steps to demonstrate your integrity and goodwill.
- Use your body language to build rapport and connect with an audience, an executive team, your staff, a prospective employer, and your clients.
- Eliminate body language that undermines your credibility and sabotages your success.
- Use your voice and language to demonstrate competence and calm rather than incompetence and stress.
- Position yourself as a thought leader with a strategic perspective.

No matter where each of us is on the continuum of personal presence, we can all improve. Personal presence is about developing your communication skills, thinking skills, and character to influence others for good and help you achieve your goals in life.

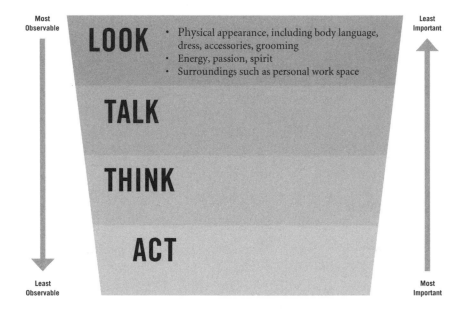

Most
Observable

LOOK
- Physical appearance, including body language, dress, accessories, grooming
- Energy, passion, spirit
- Surroundings such as personal work space

TALK

THINK

ACT

Least
Observable

Least
Important

Most
Important

PART 1: HOW YOU LOOK

1

Consider First Impressions Like First Loves

If people turn to look at you on the street,
you are not well dressed.
—BEAU BRUMMEL

The operations manager handed me two files to conduct the third and final round of interviews for a marketing specialist. "In my opinion, both are equally qualified," she said.

Caitlin's interview was scheduled first. Dressed attractively in a business suit, she walked into my office with an air of confidence well beyond her thirty years. She shook hands firmly, maintained great eye contact, smiled often, answered my questions clearly and crisply, and asked for the job before she left.

But I was predisposed to hire my second interviewee of the day, Rachel, because she came highly recommended through a colleague. She walked into my office without introducing herself and without extending her hand for the typical handshake. Disappointed, I let it pass, assuming she felt we already "knew it each other" because of the colleague's personal introduction. Younger than her competitor, she immediately gave me reason to believe that those years might make a huge difference. Although pleasant enough in her demeanor, she folded into herself. As she answered my questions about her career goals and past job, she spoke softly and sounded tentative, like a high schooler responding to the principal.

Rachel had a marketing degree and the trusted colleague had described her as "hard working, smart, and dependable." But I hired Caitlin.

Big mistake.

As it turned out, Caitlin couldn't learn the database software, had no grasp of grammar when writing email, and sported a poor customer service attitude. A few weeks later, I called Rachel back and offered her the position. Even so, I again had second thoughts when talking with her on the phone (especially when I learned that she'd been looking for work for more than a year). We immediately put her through the training programs we offer to our clients. Then because she was such a quick study and took the initiative to observe the speakers and sales professionals in and out of our offices weekly, she learned fast. Her body language changed. Her voice took on an air of authority. Within a few months she took on the role of fielding calls with major clients, speaker bureaus, and distributors. Compliments came our way almost weekly from those who spoke with her on the phone, and because of the confidence and poise she developed, literally no one would have ever guessed her age: 23. For the next several years and until she moved away, she did a great job for us.

But my point in the comparison is not Caitlin's initial confidence and Rachel's reticence. Rather, it's the critical assessment of personal presence on first meeting.

Such perceptions dictate decisions and actions every day in the world around us. Buyers make purchases based on the personal presence and persuasiveness of the salesperson. Negotiators with the strongest personal presence, not necessarily the strongest argument, walk away with the best deals.[1] People often start—or decline—a dating relationship based on first impressions. Organizations and nations often elect their leaders based on the power of personal presence as conveyed through the media.

People size you up quickly, and change their minds slowly. Researchers tell us that somewhere between eleven milliseconds and five minutes, people make judgments that do not differ from impressions made after much longer periods. So instead of resisting that fact, understand how to make it work for you rather than against you.

Yes, you can increase your presence just as Rachel did, and people *do* change their opinions of you. But the sooner you learn these skills and develop these attributes, the better. Changing impressions is not as easy as tossing away old business cards and creating a new image with different ones.

Decide what first impressions you want to last and start there.

> Changing impressions is not as easy as tossing away old business cards and creating a new image with different ones.

Take Notice of the Tangibles

You don't have to be good-looking, but that perception helps. What's good-looking? Forget movie-star looks. Here's what most cultures consider attractive: a symmetrical face, a proportionately sized body, clear skin, healthy hair, and straight teeth.[2]

Packaging and preparation can pay off handsomely. Consider the difference packaging makes in how much you're willing to pay for an item, say, software—whether the program comes on a disk with a simple black-and-white label inside a clear plastic sleeve versus the program inside a colorful well-designed package, accompanied by a brochure, instructions, and online support.

Physical attractiveness results in a fatter paycheck. Particularly, taller people earn more money than shorter people. For both men and women, a 1-inch increase brings a 1.4–2.9 percent higher paycheck. For men, a 4-inch differential in height amounts to a 9.2 percent increase in earnings.[3] According to Arianne Cohen, in *The Tall Book*, tall people earn $789 more per inch per year.[4]

Robert Cialdini also has reported significant studies in this same area: At-

> Packaging and preparation can pay off handsomely.

tractive political candidates get more votes. Attractive criminals get lighter sentences. Attractive students get more teacher attention.[5]

But wait a moment before you head off to the plastic surgeon. Although the correlation between looks and earnings has been evident for years, recent studies get to the heart of the matter: It's not *just* that beautiful people bias their bosses. Instead, the increase in wages can be attributed to three things: (1) Attractive people are more confident (about 20 percent of the cases). (2) Attractive people are considered more competent by employers—although a wrong assumption (about 30 percent of the cases). (3) Attractive people have certain skills such as communication skills and social skills that enable them to interact well (about 50 percent of the cases).[6]

Presence has much to do with perception.

All that's good news. You don't need a plastic surgeon to build confidence, teach communication, or improve your social interactions. (Besides, we'll be covering all those secrets in the following pages.)

And obviously, you can't increase your height. Presence has much to do with perception. To be perceived taller, stand tall, walk talk, and sit tall by adjusting your posture and using large gestures. Wear solid colors so you're not "cut in two" at the waist. Women, if you're wearing a jacket in a contrasting color, make sure the blouse or shell underneath matches your pants so that when the jacket hangs open, you still have the solid color from neck to ankle that elongates your appearance. Men, wear pinstripes for an elongated appearance.

As the cliché goes, attractiveness or beauty is in the eye of the beholder. Package your appearance to best advantage: good grooming; clothing styles and colors to compliment your body build, eyes, skin, hair coloring; hair styles to compliment your facial shape; makeup to compliment your natural coloring.

Know what works—and what doesn't. Here are several suggestions for help:

- Visit a good tailor. Have a good suit made and walk in with a list of questions while you're selecting fabrics and being fitted. Tailors love to share their knowledge. Let them tell you what styles work best for your body type. Ask for their recommendations about fabric and color, explaining your activities, job, and industry (travel or not, conservative or not, active or sitting all day). Ask how you can tell a quality suit from cheap imitations, and let them give you shopping pointers for accessories.
- Browse in upscale clothing stores where they have personal shoppers to assist you as you try on selections—even if you do not buy there. Ask about fit, style, and best colors for your skin tone and hair.
- Consider seeking help from an image consultant—an hour or a few hours of consulting time can do wonders. Three excellent examples are image consultants Sandy Dumont, Janice Hurley Trailor, and Valerie Sokolosky. To understand the difference clothing makes, visit a few websites for photos of this type of "makeover" (www.expertwardrobeconsultant.com for photos posted by Sandy Dumont, and www.JaniceHurleyTrailor.com for more photos). Their results are extraordinary. Several resources on both sites offer great tips on everything from ties to wingtips to nail tips. You'll also find well-qualified image consultants in your local area as well.
- Ask a trusted friend or colleague who always dresses well for their secrets and advice on your wardrobe. You probably know someone who always looks expensively dressed and well accessorized, and receives frequent compliments from colleagues. Tell them that you admire their taste and would like to know their "rules" and "taboos" for shopping and clothing selection. I guarantee they have some, and my hunch is they'll be flattered to share them with you.

Dress for Decisions

Dress for the part you want to play. Some people seem surprised to discover how much clothing counts toward the assessment of their personal competence. But think of your reaction to service repair people—those who come to your door in uniform versus those who show up in their scruffies to work on your plumbing. Anyone who has traveled extensively on an airline or stayed at a quality hotel can tell you the difference in the service they receive when they travel in expensive-looking attire versus casual clothes.

From almost two decades of coaching executives and interviewing them about their direct reports, I can tell you what diminishes their confidence in specific individuals regarding dress:

- "He wears his tie too loosely, with the collar unbuttoned underneath. And his hair feathers down on his forehead in front. He looks disheveled."
- "His fourth button on his sleeves is never buttoned. It's about attention to detail."
- "Open-toed shoes. We're a resort hotel, and I know it's hot. But she's the manager of the hotel! She knows that's not acceptable for an executive."
- "She has a very solid background. Has three hundred people reporting to her. Well-liked. But she wears wild prints at elegant affairs—rather than more classic, classy styles. She needs help with executive dress."
- "If one of my sales guys shows up in a polo, that's unacceptable. I don't care if it's a casual event at a tradeshow—I'll send him back to his hotel room for a change. If it happens a second time, he's fired."

Dress matters. Consider con artists' games. Most involve dress, a uniform of some sort that conveys authority. A police uniform. A security guard uniform. A military uniform. A business suit and all the accessories of a globe-trotting mogul. These con artists prey on the elderly, the young, and the innocent, using dress to convey credibility as they pose as some authority. A common scheme is posing as a wealthy investor looking for partners or a bank examiner asking for a confidential account number or password, sometimes even asking the victim to withdraw money from their accounts for them to help "catch the suspect." The uniform often does the trick.

In addition to dress, consider all the accessories that complete the picture: handbag, jewelry, writing instruments, briefcases. Bulging briefcases say, "I do all the work." Slim briefcases say, "I assign the work."

Gilda Radner facetiously quipped, "I base my fashion sense on what doesn't itch." You can argue that Gucci or the Gap, makeup or no makeup, hair styled or haywire, wrinkled or pressed, shined or scuffed, jeans or suits shouldn't matter. But they do.

If you're billionaire Bill Gates or Warren Buffett, you can wear what you darn well please. But until you have their stature in the business world, start the game by playing by the rules.

"But I want to be comfortable," people confide. No problem. Comfort and credibility are not mutually exclusive. In fact, those who feel uncomfortable will look uncomfortable and fidgety, losing credibility in the process. Make it your goal to dress both well and comfortably.

Research proves the importance of dress and grooming to your personal clout and credibility. Ignore it or benefit from the facts—your choice. But like it or not, people make important decisions based on your dress.

Consider the Context of Small Acts of Service

At lunch during a coaching session with Catherine, a vice president of a large aerospace manufacturer, I asked her about her rise in the organization. As we sat in her private conference room eating our salads, she related a powerful lesson learned in a male-dominated firm. The setting was the first luncheon event she'd been invited to after joining the company. She and seven male colleagues were seated around a table in a large auditorium. After the meal ended, she got up and started toward a side counter, carrying her plate.

An older waitress grabbed the plate out of Catherine's hand. "Don't you ever do that again."

"Do what?" Catherine asked her.

"Bus your own table. Doesn't look good."

At that point, as Catherine tells it, she looked around and noticed that all seven of her male colleagues had simply gotten up and walked away from the table empty-handed. Early on, she'd learned the importance of context to set image.

But there is power in serving as well as in being served—just as Catherine demonstrated in serving me lunch in her conference room that day. Image comes from just such intangible signs of personal presence. Small acts of confidence, comfort, and courtesy. Doing and saying the right thing at the appropriate moment.

Personal presence involves knowing when to serve and when to let others serve you. Service isn't about status, as the waitress wrongly assumed. But it is about courtesy, graciousness, attitude, goals, and time.

Check Your Surroundings

Personal presence extends from your workspace. When someone walks into your area and looks around, does it say, "A competent, confident person works here"? Or, does it scream, "The person working here is overwhelmed, disorganized, and incapable"?

Consider each item in your space: Coffee cups, business cards, marketing materials, reception area, walls, photos, furniture (desk, chair, rugs, pictures, lamps). High-backed chairs convey status, yet they can swallow a small person. Swivel chairs with arms give you more presence than stationary ones.

Think of it like this: You call a plumber for repairs and you expect him to have the right tools in his truck to do the job. When that's not the case, you suspect that he doesn't stay too busy and that maybe you've called the wrong guy for the job. People make the same assessments about your competence as they look at your tools and workspace.

Set the Stage to Engage

Consider how to control perceptions as you move, sit, stand, or make presentations in your workspace and in your typical meeting rooms. Research shows that where people sit in a room affects whether the listeners tune in or tune out those speaking. The farther away from the speaker, the more negative, the more confrontational, and the less recall listeners have. The closer they are to the speaker, the more engaged they become.[7]

To take advantage of this dynamic, we use the "horseshoe" seating arrangement in all Booher training programs because we want to encourage participants to interact and engage with each other as well as the facilitator. If we're going to the effort to conduct a seminar, the seating arrangement is by far the easiest thing to control for maximum impact.

Height increases presence, and you can set the stage before the discussion begins.

If you're a short person among tall colleagues, don't feel compelled to stay seated during a "sit-down" presentation. Find a reason to stand up. Wander toward the wall and adjust the thermostat. Walk to the white board and write a key word. Project a slide and point to something on the screen for a moment. Then as you return to the table, remain standing as you finish your recommendations.

In the middle of a discussion, simply stand and you'll be surprised how others will give the floor back to you because you have the height advantage. If a more aggressive colleague tends to intimidate you, make sure you offer him the lower seat on the couch and take the higher stool yourself.

If you want to increase presence in a meeting, take the seat at either end of a table. Second best seats in the house are on the left or the right of the end-of-table positions. Sitting at right angles from another person or team (rather than across the table) provides two advantages: presence and approachability. There's no barrier between you, and you're close enough to look eyeball to eyeball to increase rapport or to push back to gain more authority.

Increase Exposures to Change Opinions

You may be asking, "How can I change a first impression? That is, how can I increase my personal presence with those who already know me?"

Answer: Play the numbers.

Let me explain other interesting data from various studies on first impressions: Once people make up their mind about you, they rarely change their opinion—even when later presented with new, contradictory information.

> Consider first impressions like first loves—you rarely forget them.

Consider first impressions like first loves—you rarely forget them. That said, take them seriously. If you know first meetings will be important (as in the case of job interviews, sales calls, potential partnership discussions, key networking events), make them count. Prepare.

And if that "first love" has gone sour and you need to reestablish yourself and increase your presence in an organization, that means you need to increase exposures. Create *more* "first impressions" with new people, and create *additional* "first impressions" in new settings with your current colleagues. Let them see you in different environments, handling new projects, with increased presence. They need more time and new situations to get a different perspective.

Whenever you walk into a room, you assess the scene. Expect others to do the same. When people size you up, welcome the look-see. The goal is not calculated behavior and manipulation but rather awareness of the importance of presenting your best self. Set the stage to your best advantage, and then present yourself in the best light with multiple snapshots.

2

. . . .

Take Stage

. . . .

*The art of communication
is the language of leadership.*
—JAMES C. HUMES

Consider a dramatic scene in your favorite action-thriller movie. Let's say a missile has just hit Times Square on Tuesday at noon. Or two cars have crashed head on, burst into flames, rolled over an embankment, and landed on a cruise ship of vacationers docked in port below. Or maybe two honeymooners have decided all's fair in love and war and pulled knives on each other in the middle of the bank lobby while waiting for the cashier to open their safe deposit box.

Pick a scenario and stay with me here: Bystanders shriek. Some people scatter and duck for self-protection. Others gather and gawk at what's happening. Soon a crowd forms. Onlookers begin to shout in all directions. Chaos reigns.

Then our hero or heroine makes a way through the masses to the center of the action and takes charge: "Get an ambulance. Call the cops. Secure the site. Establish communication with headquarters." People fall in line. Chaos turns to order.

On a different note, imagine someone trying to take command of the same scene from the sidelines. In the case of the missile hitting Times Square, can you envision the crowd following orders from a SWAT commander sitting in Amarillo watching the strike on TV? Or can you picture a police officer trying to deal with the car crash scene from the comforts of the police station? How effective do you think a family member could be in breaking up the honeymooners if calling in on her cell phone from the grocery store to plead with the bride and groom to put down their weapons and cool off?

Part of your personal presence is simply being visible. That's why it's called "presence."

If you could imagine the contrasting scenes and the difficulties the out-of-pocket people might have in controlling and connecting with the crowds, you get the idea of "large and in charge." Part of your personal presence is simply being visible. That's why it's called "presence."

You increase your presence as you take up space. Literally. Of course, we can't all be as tall as my speaking colleague, Mark Eaton, formerly of the Utah Jazz. When he's collecting a group of friends in a hotel lobby to go out to dinner, there's no problem finding him in the crowd. Few people can match him at 7 feet, 4 inches and 290 pounds—on or off the basketball court.

But visibility involves much more than just height. In fact, people often say to me when we meet offstage after a keynote, "Oh, I thought you were much taller." (For the record, I'm 5'3".) Think of this issue as the opposite of the shrinking-violent syndrome. We have several clichés for this "visibility" principle: "Get in the thick of things." "If you want to lead, stay out in front."

The late Hal Persons, acting coach to some of the greatest stars of all time, used this exercise when we coached corporate presenters at IBM and elsewhere: "Pretend you're a light bulb. Push energy through the top of your head. Make the light come on." Try using that concept yourself while you talk. It makes you stand taller and radiate energy through every pore in your body!

Several years ago, the brokerage firm E.F. Hutton (now part of Citigroup) used this TV commercial with great effect: The advertisement pictured two colleagues in conversation in a public place such as a restaurant or waiting for an elevator, and one would say to the other, "My broker is E.F. Hutton, and he says . . ." People nearby overhearing the conversation suddenly stopped in their tracks to listen intently.

Can you say the same about the effect when you speak? If not, what would make it so? Consider the following ways to call people's attention as you "take the stage."

Be Front and Center

Picture the scene in a big concert hall before the program begins. The auditorium buzzes as the waiting crowd chats and hails one another across the aisles. Orchestra members tune up their instruments. Then the maestro makes a grand entrance from stage left. The crowd grows quiet. The maestro climbs onto the conductor's platform in center stage and bows to the audience. Thunderous applause as the well-wishers anticipate their entertainment for the evening. The maestro turns to face the orchestra, lifts his baton, holds it suspended in midair. Total silence.

At that moment, all eyes in the house are focused on the maestro. As the leader, he would not have the same effect directing from any position other than front and center.

The same is true of commanders in battle. The best don't *send* their troops into battle; they *lead* them into battle. That's true of leadership in any venture: Leaders with presence don't stand aside and watch what happens; they stand front and center and make it happen.

> Leaders with presence don't stand aside and watch what happens; they stand front and center and make it happen.

Project to the Cheap Seats

When you have everyone's attention, when things get quiet, when all eyes rest on you, you'll be tempted to talk to those people nearby—those people seated directly in front of you. But don't.

If you do, you'll diminish your stature. The maestro can't

afford to let his energy waver and direct only those instruments immediately in his line of sight, forcing those in the sections farther away to strain to see him. Instead, he continues to stand tall, to wave his arms at full length, to point and bring in the trombone or the double bass at exactly the appropriate moment.

You, too, will increase your presence if you continually project to those farther away from you. Rather than keeping your eyes on the friendly faces down front, talk to those seated in the back row, last seat. With those people in mind, your brain will automatically adjust your energy level, voice, and body language to project so that you can engage those people at a distance. Project your physical presence to the cheap seats far away, and those even closer will engage with you as well.

> Project your physical presence to the cheap seats far away, and those even closer will engage with you as well.

Pause Before You Launch

Talking on trajectory makes you look nervous. Whether just leaving your seat to walk to the front of a meeting room, simply rising from your chair at the conference table, or joining a conversation when someone asks your opinion, pause before you begin.

Pausing prepares you to make an assessment and take control of a situation. Scan the room or the group for a moment; consider the key interest of those you're speaking to. Never make the first words out of your mouth a throwaway line. Those meaningless mumbo-jumbo lines that people mutter at the beginning of a talk before they've put their brain in gear reflect no preparation: "Good morning. How are things going so far?" "Sorry we're a little late getting started." "This may not make much sense, but let me toss out a few ideas." Such throwaways sound like practicing your scales before the real concert begins. (For suggestions about use and placement of appropriate introductory comments of thanks and recognition of VIPs in the audience, see my earlier book *Speak with Confidence: Powerful Presentations That Inform, Inspire, and Persuade.*)

The greatest benefit of pausing is that it builds anticipation for what you have to say. A long pause says, "Here come words of great import. Listen carefully. I'm not about to just open my mouth and rattle on."

Then don't disappoint.

Presence has much to do with how *you are present. With intention, you can increase your space—both physical space and mindshare.*

3

....

Channel the Passion

....

Without passion, you don't have energy;
without energy, you have nothing.
Nothing great in the world
has been accomplished without passion.
—DONALD TRUMP

Have you ever had a friend begin to tell you about a funny weekend escapade and start laughing while telling the tale? Their amusement in setting the scene brings a smile to your face before you actually understand the crux of what happened. You're laughing along with them before they even get to the punch line of their story. In other words, it's *their amusement*—as much as their story—that creates your entertainment.

In much the same way, your passion about an idea or topic generates interest in others. You often hear it said of others, "She has a zest for life." "He has a passion for life that's contagious. You can't help but feel upbeat when you are around him." Passion refers to an intense feeling, a palpable thing. You can be passionately angry or passionately happy or passionately in love.

On the other hand, have you ever walked into someone's home and felt tension—as if everyone was "on edge" for some unknown reason? Then later, a family member explained that they'd just had an argument before your visit. As the saying goes, the tension was so thick, you could cut it with the proverbial knife.

> Those who control their passion and make it work for them have presence. Those who fail to control their passion look like excited, nervous teenagers. Those who have no passion at all have no presence.

Maybe you've even sat through similar meetings at work.

Likewise, those around you can sense your passion in your presence. It oozes through the pores of your skin and flows out in your body language.

Those who *control* their passion and make it work for them have presence. Those who *fail to control* their passion look like excited, nervous teenagers. Those who have no passion at all have no presence.

Certainly, school children are familiar with Martin Luther King, Jr.'s "I Have a Dream" speech, and public speaking classes use it as a model for many reasons. But for our purposes, consider these lines for Dr. King's passion:

> I have a dream that one day this nation will rise up and live out the true meaning of its creed: "We hold these truths to be self-evident: that all men are created equal."

> I have a dream that one day on the red hills of Georgia the sons of former slaves and the sons of former slave owners will be able to sit down together at the table of brotherhood.

> I have a dream that one day even the state of Mississippi, a state sweltering with the heat of injustice, sweltering with the heat of oppression, will be transformed into an oasis of freedom and justice.

> I have a dream that my four little children will one day live in a nation where they will not be judged by the color of their skin but by the content of their character.

Sir Ken Robinson delivered the following lines with passion (and with far less eloquence) as he spoke about his belief that schools kill kids' creativity:

They [kids] have become frightened of being wrong. And we run our companies like this, by the way. We stigmatize mistakes. And we're now running national education systems where mistakes are the worst thing you can make. And the result is that we are educating people out of their creative capacities. Picasso once said this. He said that all children are born artists. The problem is to remain an artist as we grow up. I believe this passionately, that we don't grow into creativity, we grow out of it. Or rather, we get educated out of it.[8]

But you don't have to hear the words to imagine the difference in their impact and import. Three key differences mark the degree of passion on display in our presence:

- Walk with purpose.
- Add color to your stories.
- Feel the gestures.

Walk with Purpose

Contrary to the title of Maya Angelou's classic book, people don't know why the caged bird sings—or walks. And it distracts them. So skip the nervous pacing, wandering, and foot shuffling. Some people unconsciously pace from laptop to screen to front row, to screen to front row and back repeatedly during a presentation. Others start out behind a lectern, walk to the side and rest an elbow on the edge for thirty seconds and then drop it, and return to stand behind the lectern—only to repeat the process again and again throughout their talk. Others wander from one side of the room to the opposite in an arc and then retrace their steps repeatedly for the length of their lecture.

If you asked any of these presenters why they pace, they would be unaware of their movement around the room. They do the caged pace in much the same way as other people wring their hands or clear their throat repeatedly.

Yet the pacing and foot shuffling sends a loud message to onlookers: "I am on automatic pilot. I am not present with you." Literally, while moving absentmindedly, you have lost your presence.

. . . .

Position on a platform is to a presentation what paragraphing is to a page.

. . . .

To increase the audience's sense of your presence, move purposefully. Stand still to deliver a powerful point. On the transition, walk intentionally to a new spot. Plant your feet and make your next point. Position on a platform is to a presentation what paragraphing is to a page. Your audience will feel that you are present in the moment making that point.

Add Color to Your Stories

Tell stories with gusto; put your listeners in the moment by creating scenes.

Families have their funny stories that they enjoy year after year at the expense of good-natured relatives—particularly the practical jokes played by Uncle Jerry or Grandpa Max. In our family, one of those stories centers around my mom's custom of elaborate centerpieces on the table for holiday meals.

The first year my husband and I were married, about eighteen family members gathered at my parents' home for Thanksgiving dinner. The typical compliments flowed my mother's way regarding the meal and the centerpiece, bordered by the usual tiny pieces of orange and yellow candy corn to commemorate the season.

Kevin, my practical-joker brother-in-law, said to my new husband as we sat down to dinner, "Not only does it look good; that candy tastes good, too."

Wanting to make a good impression on his mother-in-law, my husband picked up a piece of the candy corn and popped it in his mouth—and promptly broke a tooth.

The candy was plastic.

Even though it's a very brief story, did you see that happen? Did you hear the laughter (from everyone but my husband, that is)? Year after year, that story gets retold with the same amusement.

Movie directors understand the importance of setting to story—the backdrop, the costumes, the sound effects. In that same way, when you speak to a group consider your actual delivery paramount to the point. It's hard to be "larger than life" in a football stadium. By the same token, it's hard to project a calm, in-control voice while you're shouting over your cell phone from a noisy airplane.

The president spends time deciding whether to deliver a speech from the Rose Garden or the steps of an elementary school because he knows that the scene with all its detail is significant. Consider your passionate telling of a story—in scene, with details and dialogue—essential to add richness and texture to your message.

Feel the Gestures

Have you ever tried to learn a foreign language? If so, you understand the difference between those who speak a second language so fluently that they think in that language and those who have to think in their first language and then "translate" into the second language before they can speak it. Big difference. For the most part, I fall into the latter group with my second language. When I travel to South America, it takes a full week before I start to "think" in Spanish. For the first few days, it's a slow process for me to hear Spanish, translate to English, think of the English response, and then translate back and deliver the Spanish response.

People who go through that same process with gestures inevitably have a presence problem.

People who say they don't gesture when speaking have simply stifled themselves and become unnatural. In other words, they're going through a "translation" process from "natural" to unnatural. They've stripped away all the natural gestures that help convey their message. Once aware of how they're stifling or "translating" themselves for a "business" topic or setting, they understand the vast difference in the passion and energy levels between their natural self and their "unnatural" self.

Gestures are not add-ons. Gestures convey your message at the same time

Gestures are not add-ons. Gestures convey your message at the same time and with the same impact as your words. They should be part of your silent but strong vocabulary.

and with the same impact as your words. They should be part of your silent but strong vocabulary.

People with presence *feel* what they say. And that feeling comes through in their body language. How do others sense that passion?

- The speaker's face "connects" to the words—smiling, concerned, distraught, surprised, excited, disappointed, whatever.
- The speaker's posture is alert, ready to move into action, ready to respond to questions, add other information, confront, move on to other areas of interest. The speaker stands in the "ready-go" position, with weight balanced on the balls of his/her feet.
- Gestures are intentional and meaningful. The speaker gets his or her hands "out of the box." Rather than small gestures directly in front of the trunk of the body (see Figure 1), passionate gestures are sweeping: big, up, out, firm (see Figure 2). Lifting your arms from the shoulders creates a more powerful and inclusive gesture than from the elbows or wrists. In general, the bigger the room, the bigger the gesture needs to be. Gestures should not be choreographed; they happen naturally when you feel passionate about your message.

Figure 1. Small, in-the-box gestures have little impact.

Figure 2. Large, intentional gestures have strong impact.

So where's your next important conversation? An elevator? Deskside? A conference room? An airplane seat? A teleconference? A webinar screen? A hallway? An auditorium? Your enthusiastic delivery of an idea in any of these situations increases your chance to captivate others. In short, passion produces presence.

4

Translate Your Body Language to Credibility

Body language is a very powerful tool.
We had body language before we had speech.
—DEBORAH BULL

Dr. English, my father's cardiologist for the past twenty years, instinctively used his body language to support his words on two different occasions—to accomplish two opposite effects.

My dad checked into the hospital for his routine heart catheterization. I say routine because he has had five bypasses, numerous stents, and a pacemaker. They shoot the dye through his heart, identify the location and severity of the blockage, and send him home to wait until they can schedule the operating room for the surgery.

My mom, sister, and I sat in the waiting room that morning during the typical forty-five-minute procedure. "How'd it go?" I asked Dr. English when he came toward us.

"I couldn't finish. I've called in another surgeon to see if he can get in a stent."

"We didn't know you were going to do that today," my sister said.

"No choice. He wasn't going to make it. He still may not. That vein may close up at any minute. He's got only one approachable vein left, and it's open only fifteen percent."

We sat speechless for a moment, trying to take in the news. "If the surgeon . . . isn't successful, can we see him before . . . ?"

"No. You don't want to see him. It's not a pretty sight when they go this way."

"How long will the surgery take?"

"That depends. Could be fifteen minutes or five hours." Dr. English got up and walked away.

None of us questioned his decision to move ahead with the surgery or even asked who the surgeon was. With his erect posture, clipped answers, and confident tone, Dr. English had taken control of the situation. Though not exactly a compassionate bedside manner, it was certainly authoritative.

The story has a happy ending; my dad made it through the surgery. Two days later, Dr. English came by the hospital room to dismiss my dad from the hospital. My dad asked a question about his road to recovery: "I'm assuming you still want me walking my three miles a day?"

"Sure, get back out there. You don't have to walk as if you're doing a marathon, but keep at it."

"How about mowing my lawn? That still okay?"

With that question, the doctor's body language changed completely. He pulled back the blanket and sat down on the side of the bed. "Well, . . . that *might* be okay. You're not thinking of buying yourself a push mower, are you?"

My dad grinned. He and his doctor had been trading jabs for twenty years.

The doctor rubbed his chin a moment before answering. "What horsepower does it have?"

My dad told him.

"Hmmm. Well, . . ." Dr. English rubbed his chin a while longer and thumbed through the pages of his clipboard before glancing up again. "That *may* be all right. You're not planning to mow at noon during hundred-degree weather, are you?"

"Well, I might."

A few more jokes passed between them. Draping himself across the end of my dad's bed, the doctor looked so relaxed at this point that he could have been mistaken for a napping family member. Finally, he scratched his head and then drawled again, "Yeah, I guess it *might* be all right to mow if you have the right kind of mower. Just be sure to keep your nitroglycerin tablets in your pocket."

My dad hired a lawn service.

Dr. English's body language and words wove the one strong message together. The words said, "Okay, mow your lawn." The body language and hesitant tone said, "I don't think it's a good idea."

In the waiting room with family, Dr. English needed to display credibility, confidence, and competence. To his friend at bedside, he demonstrated compassion. His body language and tone delivered the appropriate message on both occasions.

What's your command of body language? Master, intermediate, or beginner?

Never Make Mediocrity the Model

Physicians tell us that 98.6 degrees is the average human body temperature. But when you visit the doctor's office for a physical, the nurse takes *your* temperature as *your* baseline. Some patients have a normal temperature of 97.25 degrees while others average 99.5 degrees when they're well.

Likewise, in our culture, we have a range of gestures, expressions, and movements that look normal for average individuals in routine situations. But people become leaders by becoming more prominent and "present" than the baseline. Their body language makes them more visible, commanding, and persuasive than others in the same situations and roles.

For models of such commanding body language, consider the leading men and women in some of your favorite movies. Watch how they stand, gesture, walk, hold their head, and use their space. These particular actors and actresses have a commanding stage presence not only in their movies, but also when they appear on talk shows, at political events, or at galas: Morgan Freeman, Brad Pitt, Matt Damon, Bruce Willis, Will Smith, Harrison Ford, Jack

Understand "normal" as a measure for mediocrity. Aim to be positively prominent. Not overwhelming, but engaging.

Nicholson, Jennifer Lopez, Julia Roberts, Sandra Bullock, Meryl Streep, Susan Sarandon, Whoopi Goldberg.

Understand "normal" as a measure for mediocrity. Aim to be positively prominent. Not overwhelming, but engaging.

A fashion consultant once admonished a colleague of mine, "Your earrings should make a statement. Get rid of those tiny little buttons, and wear earrings people can see!" The same goes for body language. Your gestures need to be large enough to matter. Where movement and gestures are concerned, beware the baseline of "normal."

Stand to Take Command

Stand with equal weight on both feet, your feet apart about the same distance as your shoulders. Keep your head in a neutral position, neither dipping it to one side nor lifting your chin. Keep your shoulders back and your stomach in. Breathe from your diaphragm. Hold yourself in this relaxed, but not rigid, posture. Stand tall. (See Figure 3.)[9]

When you need your arms and hands to make a point, use them. When you don't, drop your arms to your sides comfortably.

For the correct mindset, imagine that you're standing offstage and your name is about to be called for some high honor; you're ready to walk on stage to shake hands with the president of the United States. Take in a deep breath and

Figure 3. Commanding, yet open.

let it out. That's the ready, energized, yet relaxed, posture that looks commanding.

At times, if you want to show a little dominance—say, when a heated discussion breaks out in a meeting you're facilitating—stand in the foot-forward position. Shift your weight to one hip and the forward foot to where you need to extend control. Down through the centuries, the foot-forward was a sign of exposing your full front without a shield of protection.

Hands clasped behind the back with chest thrust forward can also be a stance of confidence—even arrogance (see Figure 4). This stance and walk is popular among royalty, military generals inspecting the troops, and police officers patrolling their beat. It looks powerful. (A tight grip on the opposite hand behind your back, however, shows frustration and even anger, as if "holding yourself back" from acting or speaking.)

Figure 4. Confident or arrogant.

Invite Others to Trust You with Open Gestures

Opening your hands and arms wide across your middle section says, "I'm open. I'm accepting you and including you in what I say. You can trust me." Keeping palms up and out says symbolically, "I have nothing to hide" (see Figure 5).

Moving your hands and arms in a calm, controlled way—rather than frantically and aggressively in an energetic appeal—comes across as objective,

Figure 5. "I'm open."

factual, and sincere. These gestures are perfect for the staff meeting when you need to put aside rumors about layoffs. Or use wide hands-and-arms gestures at waist height during an executive leadership meeting when you're giving your opinion about liability issues in pending lawsuit against your organization. These open hands-and-arms gestures also can demonstrate sincerity about providing excellent customer support after the sale when talking to a stalling prospect.

Help Others "See" What You're Saying

Comprehension improves when people literally "see" what you are saying (see Figure 6). The more content-specific gestures you use, the more the mind's eye of the listener paints a picture. For example, consider how you would gesture this message: "Sales have fallen dramatically—from a ten percent growth rate last year to only one percent this year." Consider how you would gesture this message: "In the past, . . . Currently, . . . In the future, . . ." How about

Figure 6. Content-specific gestures help people see what you're saying.

gestures for this message: "There are benefits in that. . . . On the other hand, we can't ignore the drawbacks such as . . ."? Put your body to work and "draw" the concepts visually when possible. Ideas sink in deeper when others see them as well as hear them.

Figure 7. Passionate, sincere, or aggressive appeal.

Gesturing with your hands high in front of the chest area gives the sense of a passionate, aggressive appeal (see Figure 7). Such gestures have an energetic look. The longer you hold the gesture, the more you convey the sense of "holding on" to the idea.

Walking toward others as you speak also engages and persuades more so than standing farther away.

Of course, moving into someone's personal space can be intimidating and threatening. (More about that later.)

Tension in your muscles, body language, and voice suggests to your listeners your psychological state. Because listeners reflect the speaker's state, you can move them from relaxed to neutral to alert to excited or angry just by a change in your own body language. You see this phenomenon as a political speaker moves a crowd from a logical argument to an angry chant. You feel inspired when a motivational speaker moves an audience beyond words to an emotional state so deep and quiet you can hear the proverbial pin drop. You feel excitement as the CEO challenges a small band of employees at a start-up to bring a new product to market quickly before the giant competitor crushes them.

> Moving your listeners through various psychological states from tension to relaxation of your body demonstrates tremendous personal presence.

Moving your listeners through various psychological states from tension to relaxation of your body demonstrates tremendous personal presence.

Whether dominating to take charge of a situation, increasing your presence to establish trust and credibility, or increasing your presence to persuade, keep in mind one key: congruence. If your body language says one thing and your words contradict, body language trumps. Personal presence is first and foremost about the physical.

5

Don't Disappear

Our expression and our words never coincide,
which is why the animals don't understand us.
—MALCOLM DE CHAZAL

As a lengthy consulting project ended, the CEO of the client organization took me out to dinner to celebrate. During the meal, he asked, "Is there anybody on my team who you think deserves special recognition? I believe in giving strokes where they're due. Obviously, Norm and Najma were key players. But who else have I overlooked?"

"Well, now that you ask—Wayne has really impressed me with both his competence and his commitment."

"Who?"

"Wayne." I had to give him the last name.

"Really." The CEO looked as if he were punching the information into his brain and receiving only error messages. The readout told him Wayne in Editorial couldn't possibly be a key player.

Granted, Wayne lacked physical presence. He meandered as he moved from studio set to set. He slouched over his workspace as he edited scripts. His voice sounded weak, as if he'd been awakened in the middle of the night under duress. He dressed like the mad mathematician—checkered shirt, striped tie, and leather-patch elbows on his corduroy jacket.

"Wayne? Hmmm. Really." The CEO mumbled again to himself.

Being an outsider and not knowing whether I was stepping into a political minefield, I took the chance to sing Wayne's praises. I waxed on about his scriptwriting talent and his negotiating abilities in keeping all the actors happy with the many script changes.

The CEO nodded as I finished. "That's good to know. You just don't notice people like Wayne because they're so . . . so unassuming. They do their job and keep their head down. But that's good to hear about Wayne. I'll have to take care of him in his next paycheck."

But what happens to the Waynes of the world when someone else is not around to make them visible? What causes them essentially to disappear from the view and consciousness of those around them?

Congruency Is Key

Sending a mixed message diminishes personal presence. A physical presence overpowers a psychological one. And when the two conflict, confusion results in the listener's brain. (For example, if you speak boldly, but your physical presence seems unassuming, that weak physical presence becomes the stronger message.) Congruence is essential to clear communication and a strong personal brand.

As noted previously, authenticity in all areas increases presence.

Forget trying to fake your face. You can't do it. Not according to Dr. Paul Ekman, who has been studying facial expressions for more than forty years among cultures all over the world. (You may have seen the TV series *Lie to Me*, which is based on his work.) Facial expressions are created with more than 52 facial muscles and the associated nerves and blood vessels woven around the bone structure. Those components can morph into more than 5,000 expressions that signal others about what's going on inside your mind.[10]

Recently, I had a chance to check out Dr. Ekman's thesis personally. At an industry meeting I attended, the speaker asked us to pair ourselves with someone we didn't know. She then asked us to introduce ourselves and take three minutes to discuss a specific issue. Immediately, I felt reluctant about the interaction because I considered the issue proprietary information that I didn't feel comfortable sharing with competitors.

A woman from an adjoining table stepped over beside me. We shook hands. She said, "Okay, I'll go first. My name's Robin. I'm a psychologist specializing in criminal behavior. Right now I'm working with the TSA, training staff to spot terrorists."

Then she added, "And I see fear just now on your lower face." She was absolutely correct. It was not that I intended to blow up any planes. But I did feel instant fear. Fear from having someone read my face. Fear from feeling so transparent, vulnerable, and unmasked. What if she saw my reluctance to share the competitive information? She read it all in a second without my realizing that I'd moved a muscle. In fact, I kept my smile, but to her, as a professional body-language expert, it must have looked like a Halloween mask.

> Forget trying to fake your face.

Though not as proficient as Robin, others around us sift through the fake to focus on the core message. So forget it—you can't fake your face. Be congruent.

Beware Body Language That Rules You Out

Consider the following examples of negative body language that diminishes your presence. At best, the various gestures may reveal secrets you don't want to communicate.

"I'm a Loser": Slouching posture suggests defeat (see Figure 8). It mimics what small animals do when larger animals drive them away from food. They hang their head forward or sideways, look downward, and lean on first one and then the other foot or slink away as if dismissed. The look says, "Poor, poor, pitiful me. Please feel sorry for me. I can't help myself." The trunk of the body seems to cave in on itself, and the arms and hands make

Figure 8. "I'm a victim."

tiny gestures inside an invisible box. Often, these people duck away from others and sit in the dropout zone in meetings—the empty chairs around the edge of the wall—or sit or stand in other spaces away from the action in any gathering. All this completes the picture of defeat.

"I'm Nervous; I Need Reassurance": Some gestures show signs of inward stress (see Figure 9). They relieve tension building up on the inside: smoking rituals, gum-chewing, nail-biting, finger-tapping, foot-tapping or -shuffling, hair-tossing, sleeve- or cuff-link adjusting, watch-band adjusting, lint-picking, ring-twisting, necklace-fondling, knuckle-cracking, button-adjusting, coffee-cup shuffling, leg-twining, hugging yourself (one arm grasping the other and hugging it tightly to the trunk of the body), hands rubbing neck, holding your own hands in front of you or behind you (in imitation of having a parent hold your hand) (see Figure 10).

Figure 9. "I'm nervous."   Figure 10. "Hold my hand, Mommy."

When you stand to speak or walk, a few more gestures scream "I lack confidence": pacing, waving your hands frantically and randomly, crossing one or both arms across the chest for protection, locking your arms behind your back, clasping your hands tightly in front of or behind you. Some people clutch props such as a handbag, port-folio, or file folder in front of themselves for protection as they

Figure 11. "I'm holding my shield for protection."

walk nervously in front of a group (see Figure 11).

"I'm Impatient": Consider the impact of a head nod. When listening, your nod says, "I understand what you're saying." Speed marks the difference between a welcome nod and dismissive nod. Three or four slow, deliberate nods say, "You're making a good point." But fast nodding says, "Enough! Finish already!" Or: "Let me have a turn to talk." Big difference between "welcome" and "enough!"

"I Feel Defensive and Argumentative": One leg crossed comfortably over the other feels and looks normal to seventy percent of the population—in European, Asian, and British cultures. But you'll see the Figure Four in America (one leg crossed over the other knee so that the legs form the numeral 4) and in any culture that is becoming Americanized through travels, TV, and movies (see Figure 12). According to body language experts Allan and Barbara Pease, because the Figure Four exposes the genital area, it says, "I'm feeling strong, dominate. I disagree. I feel like arguing your point."[11] With legs crossed, the meaning is just the opposite: a closed, defensive attitude (see Figure 13). When someone crosses both arms and legs, they're emotionally checked out of the conversation.

Putting your hands in your pockets, the exact opposite of open palms,

Figure 12. Comfortable and open.

Figure 13. Closed and defensive.

Figure 14. Disengaged.

Figure 15. "Not on my watch, you aren't!"

Figure 16. "I could do that in five minutes— not exactly brain surgery."

says the same thing: "I don't want to engage in this conversation. I'm checking out" (see Figure 14).

"I'm Angry": With chin down, you're showing negativity or disapproval (see Figure 15). As the attitude or emotion grows stronger, arm gestures grow more staccato. Or, if you're angry, you may do the opposite: Resort to the silent treatment, pout, withdraw, cut yourself off physically from others (sit away from others at meetings, point your body away, block out open spaces with your belongings so that no one else can sit near you). Feel this emotion long enough, and your mouth may morph into what's called a permanent down-mouth—much like what the bulldog wears.

"I'm Arrogant": The universally recognized gesture of arrogance is the raised chin (see Figure 16). We frequently hear the cliché, "He walked by with his nose in the air." It signifies a smug attitude. Another most-hated male display is the cluster gesture: hands-behind-the-head, with Figure-Four legs. Symbolically, it leaves the frontal area totally exposed, saying, "I'm totally confident." Women most often read it, "I'm totally cocky." Use it at your peril.

Jutting your chin out at someone says, "I see you and recognize you, but I'm not bothering to speak."

Figure 17.
Self-assured.

Figure 18.
"Whatever."

Figure 19.
"I'm making it up as
fast as I can . . ."

Steepling hands—either in front of your chest, in front of your face, or in your lap—suggest a self-assured attitude and even superiority (see Figure 17).

"You're Crazy": The sarcastic eye roll or eye shrug as in "whatever" so typically delivered from teens to their parents conveys boredom, sarcasm, frustration, or lack of respect (see Figure 18).

"I'm Lying Now, So You Can't Trust Other Things I Say Either": Consider some small lies tactful (such as responses to "How do you like my haircut?"). Other lies lead to growing doubt for important messages, and over time they diminish trust and personal credibility. So what are the signs of lying? Sweating. Flushing. Increased swallowing. Irregular breathing. Hand-to-mouth and hand-to-nose touching (see Figure 19). Either frequent blinking or a stare (the opposite of what's typical for the person). The frozen face (an attempt to be expressionless and not give away any secrets).

Figure 20.
"Let me tell you
a thing or two."

"Do As I Say Or Else!": Pointing your fingers or gesturing with your hands or palms down almost always sends a negative message: "Listen to me. I'm the authority here" (see Figure 20). When I do speaking tours through Malaysia, the Philippines, Singapore, and China, one of the first things my sponsors always remind me of

Figure 21. "I'm
attracted to you."

Figure 22. "I want your approval.
How am I doing?"

Figure 23. "Don't you think
I'm cute?"

this: "Remember to use your entire hand when you point. Point-ing with your finger is an insult."

"I'd Rather Flirt Than Talk Business": Whether subconsciously or intentionally, women suggest their femaleness by glancing over a raised shoulder (see Figure 21). Or, they dip their head to the side and peep upward (see Figure 22). When speaking, this head tilt is a submissive gesture that makes a person look smaller and more vul-nerable. (When listening, however, the head tilt to the side can be positive, showing openness.)

When women feel attracted, they often expose the inside of their wrist and display the silky smooth skin there (see Figure 23). Men tuck their thumbs into their belt or into the tops of their pockets—just as you see in the TV Westerns when the gunslingers dare each other to see who's the better man. The gesture frames their frontal area (see Figure 24). Both genders use the hands-on-hips gesture (the aggres-sive, readiness gesture) to say, "Look at me." Women often add the pelvic tilt to this hands-on-hip gesture (think fashion model on the catwalk) to say, "Look at me!" (see Figure 25).

Figure 24. "Look at me!
What a man, huh?"

Figure 25. "Look at me.
Aren't I sexy?"

Handle the Handshake with Precision

The normal handshake involves grasping another person's hand firmly, holding it so that both palms are parallel, giving the hand two to four pumps, and then releasing it. Variations on this normal handshake are negative, ranging from noticeably negative to nerve-wracking.

The Dead-Fish: Offering limp, lifeless fingers for someone to try to grasp and shake.

The Macho-Man: Offering the vise-grip and applying pressure as if you're in a competitive contest to bring them to their knees with cracked bones.

The Lover's Clasp: Covering their hand with both of yours as if it's the beginning of . . . what?

The Dominator: Clasping their hand and then twisting the palms so that your hand actually rests on top with theirs on the bottom. For added dominance, some people push the hands toward the other person's stomach, giving themselves the real "upper hand."

The Double-Grab: Grabbing the other's hand in a normal way, but with the second hand, grabbing the receiver's wrist, or elbow, or upper arm, or shoulder. These all show intimacy and possessiveness that may offend.

Do handshakes matter? An acquaintance of mine, a former Secret Service agent who stands 6'3" and weighs more than 200 pounds tells about a conversation he once had with a union business agent: "The guys like you, but you have a weak handshake. They *respect* a firm handshake." In his line of work, a conversation like that will get your attention.

Avoid getting a relationship off on the wrong foot with a handshake that speaks louder than your words about your personality, intentions, and attitude.

Smile at Your Own Risk or Reward

Studies at both the Uppsala University in Sweden and University College in London suggest that the brain triggers a reaction in our facial muscles that is partly responsible for the recognition of facial expressions and causes an instantaneous mirroring reaction.[12] As a result of this brain programming, your smiling at others directly influences their reaction to you. That is, a smile brings on a smile.

Smiling is also a submissive gesture; it tells others you're non-threatening. Remember the Westerns: "Who comes there—friend or foe?" A friendly smile says, "Just me. See, I'm smiling. No harm intended." No smile says to the other person, "I'm dominant, not submissive." That interpretation could be the reason certain political figures and character actors rarely smile.

Lack of smiling can also give you a tense, worried, even angry look. So to paraphrase Hamlet, "To smile or not to smile, that is the question."

I recall coaching a vice president, Greg, about the fact that his smiling had become detrimental to his job. The CEO had told me that Greg smiled inappropriately—when testifying before Congress, when presenting a proposal to clients, when entertaining foreign dignitaries. When I met Greg for the first time, his smile was the first thing I noticed. His entire face brightened, and crow's feet spread from his eyes to his hairline. It was an infectious, genuine grin that I couldn't help but reflect.

So what was the problem? According to his CEO, when Greg smiled, congressional members judged him to be flippant or sarcastic, customers considered his smile a condescending response to them and their concerns, and foreign dignitaries assumed he was amused at their mistakes in speaking a second language.

Did you ever hear a parent or teacher reprimand a child, and hear them say with an annoyed tone, "Wipe that silly grin off your face?" To Greg's boss, his smile seemed exaggerated and inappropriate.

Do keep in mind that interpretation can be regional. Karen, a friend of mine, tells of a comment from her twelve-year-old grandson one day after she moved to Natchitoches, Louisiana, and bought The Steel Magnolia House bed-and-breakfast (made famous from the movie). The grandson said to Karen, "I think you should run for governor."

"Governor? Why is that?"

"Everybody in the state knows you."

"Why do you think that?"

"Everybody smiles and speaks to you."

In the South, smile at someone and they return the smile and speak. (Remember the ribbing George W. Bush took for his grin?) In the North, smile at someone, and they wonder what no-good you've been up to or what you want.

Smiling—there's an app for that. It's called situational appropriateness.

Smile when you're pleased, when you agree, or when you're acknowledging someone. Smiling is inappropriate when you're suppressing anger or disagreement, when you're giving bad news, or when you're offering sympathy. Smiling at the wrong time can convey ignorance or an attitude of superiority, arrogance, or scorn.

So what do you do if your body language betrays you? Psychologists insist that you can't feel your way into new body language habits. Instead, they recommend that you act your way into a new feeling. In other words, to *feel* confident, use confident body language. If you don't *feel* comfortable controlling a conversation, *act* confident in facilitating conversations to a decisive close. As a result, you'll start to *feel* comfortable in that role.

Practice in low-risk settings with colleagues you trust to give you honest feedback. Before a big client meeting or an important presentation for your boss, pull some friends together for a dry run followed by feedback. Give them a checklist of principles from this book, and ask for an honest assessment of your body language. Or, better yet, record the entire dry run and critique yourself.

Drop the loser body language that causes others to dismiss you. Replace it with confident body language until you feel competent in whatever role you undertake. The principle? Look like a leader to feel like a leader.

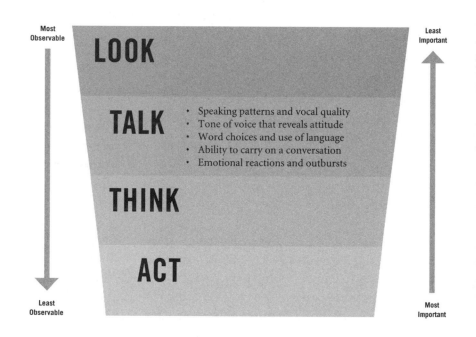

Most Observable

Least Important

LOOK

TALK
- Speaking patterns and vocal quality
- Tone of voice that reveals attitude
- Word choices and use of language
- Ability to carry on a conversation
- Emotional reactions and outbursts

THINK

ACT

Least Observable

Most Important

PART 2: HOW YOU TALK

6

. . . .

Be Professional, Not Professorial

. . . .

Words are like eyeglasses;
they blur everything that they do not make clear.
—JOSEPH JOUBERT

An acquaintance of mine, Troy, can shut down a party quicker than a police raid. Worse, he has no intention of doing so.

Take last Sunday afternoon for an example. About thirty of us gathered at a local golf club after church for a leisurely lunch. Seated on both sides of two long tables, first one and then another opened a new discussion topic. "What are you thinking about the elections?" Two or three jumped in with opinions. Then Troy. "You have to look at this upcoming election historically." He waxed on for two or three minutes, providing historical "significance" for the elections rather than mere opinion.

Then someone asked for an update on the investigation into the latest terrorist threat. Troy gave a full report, including how-tos on prevention. Someone changed the subject to the latest movies. You guessed it: Troy gave us a lengthy rundown on all the reviews, told us which reviewers were most credible, explained how the movie got its funding, and ended with how much money the average movie made over its lifetime. By the fourth time Troy had hijacked the conversation to "explain" things to us, a deadly pall had fallen over the table. One by one, guests left the table to form smaller chat groups around the room.

As I said, Troy can disperse a crowd faster than a deranged gunman—with only his mouth loaded. A *little* expertise engages—just not on *every* topic.

Be conversational, but not captivating. Okay, if you're dating, aim for captivating in the charming sense of the word. But otherwise, don't take prisoners. Those around you should not feel trapped when you talk.

Lessons learned from Troy? Just because you *know* something doesn't mean you have to *say* something. If the thought occurs that you may be rambling on too long, you are. If people often cut you off with, "I've got it," you're probably being repetitive.

If you see eyes glaze over, you've lapsed into lecture mode and lost your audience. As T.S. Eliot observed, "Words strain, crack, and sometime break, under the burden." Heavy users should have to pay a licensing fee when they exceed their limit.

Stake Your Claim to State Your Opinion

Watching the occasional TV program, I often feel sorry for guests trapped on talk shows who haven't learned to hold their own long enough to state their views. Others interrupt them to the point that it appears someone hit their "mute" button and shut them down. On a panel in a seven-minute time slot, a panelist can disappear after the first go-around unless the moderator saves them by tossing a question to them by name.

To hold your own and keep this from happening to you, set yourself up to hold the floor from the outset. In a meeting with someone who habitually interrupts, speak in a firm voice and state your framework to signal others where you intend to go: "Let me point out three reasons I think we should reconsider funding this project. . . ." If the interrupter butts in after reason one, continue in a firm voice, "Please let me finish with my other two reasons. . . ." and continue.

Stake your claim to hold the floor. Refuse to be rudely interrupted.

Choose Not to Lose with Your Words

Adjectives and adverbs express opinions and therefore invite people to nitpick and argue. Use them sparingly. Verbs and nouns express facts (or what sound like facts). Verbs motivate, persuade, and demand action. They pack punch. (Turn back to the beginning of Chapter 2 for an extended passage of strong action-packed verbs.)

> **Weak:** This *outdated* law *somewhat* hinders our progress in making the *necessary* changes.
> **Stronger:** This law hinders our progress in making changes.

Jargon, too, can be troublesome. Often, people use jargon in an attempt to impress or build rapport as an insider with extensive knowledge. But instead of building rapport, jargon builds a barrier. Rather than marking you as a leader with broad knowledge who can identify with everyone, jargon categorizes you as a specialist with limited perspective.

Adam Freedman, attorney and columnist for the *Wall Street Journal*, tells of a lesson he learned early on as a young associate, representing a prisoner in a civil-rights case. The first draft of his argument began, "Plaintiff John Doe is currently serving a custodial sentence in the New York State penal system." The partner of the firm took out his red pen and edited his opening this way: "John Doe is a prisoner at Sing Sing." Mr. Freedman confesses that the experience ended his effort to try to dazzle with jargon.[13]

Several years ago, I attended a conference where the luncheon speaker pulled a colossal gag on the group. The emcee stepped to the microphone to introduce Dr. So-and-So, a world-renowned specialist on the science of communication. After a lengthy recitation of his biography, including academic credentials, publications, and awards, the keynoter walked to the lectern and began his talk. He cited study after study and referred to research project after project, using jargon, complex terminology, and convoluted explanations.

Energy evaporated from the typically bustling crowd of about

2,000 people. Members of the audience listened politely for about ten minutes, and then they began to give each other sideways glances across the luncheon tables, as if to ask, "Are you following any of this?" "Are we trapped here for forty-five minutes?" At about the ten-minute mark, a few chuckles began to break out and the whispers became, "Is this guy for real?"

He wasn't.

The whole bit was a ruse—part of comedian Rodney Marks' (www.comedian.com.au) act to satirize double-speak and see how long the audience would sit there and listen to nonsense, meaningless jibber-jabber and jargon without protest. Answer: A long time. But not with reason and respect. And not thinking what you'd want them to be thinking.

Jargon is definitely not the language leaders use to engage. Instead, edit yourself. As professor and author William Strunk observed, "A sentence should have no unnecessary words, a paragraph no unnecessary sentences, for the same reason that a drawing should have no unnecessary lines and a machine no unnecessary parts."

Profound people strive for simplicity and clarity.

> "Simplicity is the ultimate sophistication."
> —LEONARDO DA VINCI

Booher's Rules for Clear Communication

1. Strive for simplicity. Never use a long word when a short word will do.

2. Express your core idea with strong verbs and precise nouns.

3. Use active voice, unless you have a good reason for passive voice.

4. Stick with standard words instead of coining new words.

5. Check word usage and pronunciation.

6. Be prepared, but not canned. Talk, don't recite. If people want to hear a script, they'll go to a Broadway play or watch a documentary.

7. Speak fluidly, not haltingly.

8. Don't let diction and dialect detract.

9. Speak up, then shut up.

Let me elaborate on a couple of these.

Don't Let Diction and Dialect Detract

When I was nineteen, I enrolled in the University of Maryland, Far East Division, on the military base in Okinawa for a couple of semesters. As a civilian attending my first class there, I felt a little shy seated in a lobby waiting area alone on the first evening of enrollment. A soldier passed directly in front of me and tripped on my feet. He excused himself; I nodded and responded with, "Hi."

"What part of Texas are you from?" he asked as he sat down beside me.

"How did you know I was from Texas?"

"How many other people make two syllables out of 'Hi'?"

He had me there. The southern drawl is a dead giveaway of my origins. I've since traveled and spoken to audiences in almost all fifty states and on six continents, and invariably people recognize the Southern accent. Almost every area of the country has its regional dialect and all the prejudices that go with it. Some from the North consider the stereotypical slow pace of the South a sign of ignorance. Some from the South consider the stereotypical fast-talkers from the North pushy and slick.

Those dialectic variations make us individuals and add variety from speaker to speaker.

But the things that raise eyebrows like fingernails scratching a chalkboard include matters of diction, misused words, and poor grammar.

"Irregardless of the cost, this project should be completed."

"Send that report to Lisa, Himanshu, and myself."

"Me and Jeri have made our plans to attend."

"The team worked real good together."

"He had went to work that morning the same as always." (When I mentioned this error in *Booher's Rules of Business Grammar*, I actually had someone tell me: "That must be an error only made in the South among the uneducated because I've never heard anyone in the North say that." Every time an engineer or systems analyst with an advanced degree from a client organization in the North makes the error, I'm tempted to forward the document to her.)

"The convention is gonna be in Warshington."

Check Word Usage and Pronunciations: How's That Again?

Comedian Norm Crosby made a living with malapropisms. The term malapropism refers to the mistake of using a different word than the speaker or writer intends. The term actually originated from Richard Sheridan's 1775 play *The Rivals*, in which the character Mrs. Malaprop frequently misspoke, to great comic effect. Example: "What are you incinerating?" meaning "What are you insinuating?"

Mispronunciations can be equally embarrassing. Unless you intend to make comedy your day job, these can stall your career.

Certain common words have syllables that people routinely transpose. And once learned incorrectly, these words become dragons to slay. Here's a starter list. Because even your best friend won't tell you, check these for yourself to create awareness.

relevant (re-le-vant, often mispronounced *re-ve-lant)*

remuneration (re-mu-ner-a-tion, often mispronounced *re-nu-mer-a-tion)*

nuclear (nu-cle-ar, often mispronounced *nuke-cu-lar* as in *particular) candidate (can-di-date* often mispronounced *can-ni-date)*

escape (es-cape, often mispronounced *ex-cape)*

jewelry (jew-el-ry, often mispronounced *jew-le-ry)*

supposedly (sup-pos-ed-ly, often mispronounced *sup-pos-a-bly)*

asterisk (as-ter-risk, often mispronounced *as-te-rix, as-ter-icks)*

mispronunciation (mis-pro-nun-ci-a-tion, often mispronounced *mis-pro-noun-ci-a-tion)*

mischievous (mis-chie-vous, often mispronounced *mis-chee-ve-ous)*

February (Feb-roo-air-y, often mispronounced *Feb-yoo-air-y)*

plenitude (plen-i-tude, often mispronounced *plent-i-tude)*

across (a-cross, often mispronounced *a-crost)*

oriented (o-rient-ed, often mispronounced *o-rien-tated)*

often (of-fen, often mispronounced *of-ten)*

library (li-bra-ry, often mispronounced *li-berry)*

I can tell you from experience that it feels far better to make yourself aware of such mistakes than to let others do it for you. Two decades ago in speaking to a group of lawyers at an oil and gas company, I referred to a passage in one of their documents that used the term *subsidence* and put the accent on the wrong syllable. A lawyer in the group glared over the top of his glasses and in a very superior tone corrected me. My face almost flushes again just to remember the situation.

Do you recall the incident in November 2010 when a very wrinkled elderly Caucasian man boarded an Air Canada flight in Hong Kong headed for Vancouver, wearing a hat and cardigan, went into the toilet onboard, and then emerged as a twenty-something Asian? The news media carried the story and photos for days while the FBI investigated how he slipped through security checkpoints, trying to enter the country illegally. Some had noticed that the young-looking hands didn't fit the rest of his body.

Inspectors tell us they look for similar discrepancies when deciding whom to question: Someone dressed in a business suit, but with dirty fingernails. A mother with children, but unable to remember their birth dates. A woman in a business suit, but with scuffed shoes. These out-of-sync pictures signal deception—that something's not quite as it appears on the surface.

The same out-of-sync image occurs when someone with an otherwise striking physical presence butchers the King's English. The language jars our perception and first reaction to the person.

Tackle Taboo Topics with Caution

"You can dress him up, but you can't take him out." Typically, that one-liner refers to a friend who has accidentally knocked over a beverage at the dinner table or dribbled mustard on his shirt. But it also applies to the lack of sensitivity about what topics are appropriate on which occasions. Watching an out-of-control mouth rush in where fools fear to tread creates the same apprehension as watching a drunk at a party. You stand by thinking, "Somebody should tape his mouth and drive him home safely."

> Watching an out-of-control mouth rush in where fools fear to tread creates the same apprehension as watching a drunk at a party. You stand by thinking, "Somebody should tape his mouth and drive him home safely."

Someone once observed that lower class people talk about other people. Middle class people talk about things. Upper class people talk about ideas. In my experience, choice of topics doesn't have so much to do with class as leadership and a sense of self. People without a strong sense of self talk about other people because, stuck in comparison mode, they focus on how they stack up against others. Those with a somewhat greater sense of self become selfish. They focus on how the world revolves around them and theirs. Those with the strongest sense of self focus outward.

Leaders with presence talk about ideas. Talking about suitable topics intelligently reflects a broader interest: struggles on the world scene, new technology, feeding the poor, the latest medical research, survey results on fitness, current books.

You're known by the topics you tackle. Bringing up your uncle's decayed wisdom tooth at the lunch table causes people to question your judgment.

Discretion about what kind of humor is appropriate and what's not also affects stature.

A couple of years ago, I was asked to deliver the eulogy at a friend's funeral. She was a small business owner relatively new to the community where she'd moved just before being diagnosed with a terminal illness. As eulogies go, mine was a lengthy one intended to be the bulk of the service. I described her as an accomplished businesswoman, a committed Christian who had served others selflessly, a loyal friend, a devoted mother, and a loving wife.

Then the officiating minister asked others in the large crowd if anyone would like to stand and say a word or two of remembrance—either a serious or funny story about Jenny. Many wonderful memories were shared. But one comment I recall particularly. A young woman in her early twenties stood and said, "She sure did enjoy bathroom humor." The remark fell like a bowling ball, revealing much more about the discretion of the speaker than the deceased.

The perception of presence is not only about the company you keep but the words you speak.

7

Heed the
Highlighter Principle

He had occasional flashes of silence
that made his conversation perfectly delightful.
—SYDNEY SMITH

"Let me get this straight: These seventeen executives will be flying in just to prepare for the awards banquet?"

"That's right." Cyndi, director of communications, nodded to me about my upcoming coaching assignment. "Since this is Corporate, some may try to schedule other meetings while they're here—to see Garrett or Boyd. But they know Garrett wants them here for this coaching primarily. Last year's banquet was terrible. Garrett was embarrassed. Spending this much money on all the awards to make this a special night for the recipients and their families, we've got to do it right."

"I understand." We walked into the studio to meet the president of the production company they'd hired and a few of his crew on hand for the practice session.

The scriptwriter walked over to introduce himself and give me a copy of the script. "Just give us any changes you want as we go, and we'll input them into the teleprompter."

A movie producer friend of mine always said there are three essentials to a great movie: (1) The script, (2) the script, and (3) the script. And at this point, I was growing more and more tense because I had not yet had an opportunity to read this script, and my first executive was arriving at 8:00 a.m. for his coaching session on the set. I sat down at the makeshift desk at the back of the studio to review the lines. Thumbing through the pages quickly, I pulled up the VP's segment. Only two short paragraphs? This was it?

I found Cyndi talking to the production crew. "Excuse me, but is this the total script for Curtis—two paragraphs?"

"That's it."

"And it's on the teleprompter?"

"It is."

"And we have an hour together to work on this?"

She smiled. "I know what you're thinking. But believe me, you'll need the time. Maybe not with all of them. But with most."

She was right. I had them deliver their lines from a hard copy first before tackling the teleprompter. But it wasn't just the teleprompter that gave the executives trouble. They simply didn't realize that they talked in a monotone. That is, they weren't aware of the problem until they listened to the video recording of themselves. Then it became excruciatingly painful to them.

Sarah has been instrumental in the . . . development of several key policy . . . manuals here at Universal. In fact, around . . . here, we call her the Energizer Bunny . . . because she and her team have . . . interviewed, researched, coded and . . . distributed more than 19 online . . . reference guides. When not . . . working, Sarah and her husband . . . enjoy mountain . . . biking with their twins and . . .

On and on, their voices droned, sputtered, and stopped like a sluggish engine on a cold morning. Not only did they phrase inappropriately, as if reading; it was as if someone had sucked the breath out of them. They seemed unaware that their voices mimicked those telemarketers calling at the dinner hour with the opening line, "May I speak to the head of the household please?"

Five minutes into the session, these normally energetic junior vice presidents, typically working sixty-hour weeks, sounded like deflated tires.

So how did they—and how does anyone—learn to project personal presence with their voice? That's a question worth asking, according to our survey. When it comes to personal presence, only two percent of the Booher survey respondents considered their voice their strongest attribute.

Change Your Body Language to Master the Monotone Monster

Your voice follows your body—not the reverse. Voice quality involves breathing properly. You can't breathe properly if you don't stand properly. Without standing properly, you can't inhale to full lung capacity. Without taking enough air into your lungs, you can't breathe out enough air to talk with the intensity needed to sound strong and energetic. So stand up straight, expand your lungs, and take in enough air so you can speak with energy and force behind your words.

The message happens in the listener's head. When there's an incongruent message, listeners believe the voice quality and tone they hear—not the words coming out of your mouth.

When the systems engineer says, "We've found the coding problem. You shouldn't have any more downtime" with a furrowed brow and soft voice, the manager hears, "I'm not sure the problem has been handled." When the CFO tells Wall Street analysts, "The pending lawsuit is just a nuisance threat and will never go to court," they're listening to voice quality for confidence. If Colonel Herzog announces, "Soldiers, the Pentagon has just signed the paperwork to make your raises official," but the message comes wrapped in a monotone, the troops will expect bad news to follow.

Nowhere does voice quality become more apparent than when the listener already feels fatigued. Consider a child's bedtime. It's not the bedtime story that puts them to sleep; it's the quiet tone of voice that shuts their eyes and causes them to fade out. Consider a plane ride. It's the monotonous drone of the airplane engine that puts passengers to sleep on long flights.

Make sure the surroundings (your caved-in body) don't force you into a low-energy monotone.

Become the Highlighter, If Not the Headliner

Consider the highlighter principle to increase your presence. If you're studying for the bar exam or the CPA exam, my guess is that you'd use a yellow highlighter (or pink, green, or orange maybe) to mark key ideas in your notes, articles, and books so they stand out as you review. As a lawyer, you'd be highlighting case names, dates, and judicial rulings that set case precedent. As an accountant, you'd be highlighting formulas, IRS regulations, and various court rulings on tax cases.

When speaking, your voice inflection acts as that highlighter for the listener. You punch (inflect, emphasize) those words harder with volume and intensity; you pause before and after them longer so that they stand out from the rest of the sentence. Your listeners have neither a script nor a highlighter to follow along as you speak; your vocal variation must mark key ideas for their attention and recall.

> Your listeners have neither a script nor a highlighter to follow along as you speak; your vocal variation must mark key ideas for their attention and recall.

Most people highlight well in casual conversations—about the movie they saw last weekend, their favorite football team, or the current project that has them puzzled. Consider the following comment and how the meaning changes with each variation, depending on which word I highlight or emphasize:

"The CLIENT didn't say Robert was upset about the decision."
"The client DIDN'T say Robert was upset about the decision."
"The client didn't SAY Robert was upset about the decision."
"The client didn't say ROBERT was upset about the decision."

"The client didn't say Robert was UPSET about the decision."
"The client didn't say Robert was upset about the DECISION."

Highlighting conveys meaning on most occasions. To practice, read book or article passages aloud to a family member. See if they grasp ideas or information easily or instead get confused and ask you to reread. Practice highlighting until you master the monotone monster.

Recharge Your Voice with Movement

When presenters stand in one spot to address a group, they often lose all sense of natural inflection, pacing, and pausing. They lapse into a monotone, and the sound pales to pathetic. Don't let that happen to you.

Stay conscious of the link between your energy and your lips. Learn to modulate your speaking rate, your volume, and your intensity so that your listeners know what's important. Make others feel your energy as you drive home a key point. Let them rest a bit, then pick up the pace again. Move. Walk to a different spot in the room to deliver a new point. Use the entire conference room as your platform. When appropriate, gesture with your entire body. Become your own prop when you need one. Use your hands. Animate your face. Get the blood flowing. Movement takes energy. The more energy you exert as you move, the more energetic and natural your voice will sound.

> Stay conscious of the link between your energy and your lips.

Modulate, modulate, modulate. If your listeners look bored, it's because you *sound* boring!

"The lack of a strong personal presence projected through the voice during a telephone interview keeps many executives from getting the second job interview," according to Sharon Reedie, president of Costrata Management in Dallas. In her more than twenty years in helping executives throughout the nation conduct confidential job searches, she finds that the biggest mistake made by even the most sophisticated executives has been to take the phone interview too casually. Their cell phone rings while they're on the way to the grocery store or at the golf club and they answer it, unprepared. What they *should* do when they don't recognize the number, Reedie explains, is call back when they're prepared to answer questions. Preparation leads to confidence, and confidence comes across in a strong voice.

Deborah, a candidate with whom Reedie had just begun work, has a great sense of humor, a vibrant personality, and a strong physical presence. But these traits did not come across in her recent executive job interview done by phone. Deborah took the call as she waited in line to pick up her children from school. The hiring executive perceived her as "flippant," "drab," "nervous," "too detailed," and "uninterested in the job." None of these adjectives describe the real candidate—but that's the personality her voice projected at the moment: low energy, mousy, uninteresting. Her monotone voice projected a monotone personality. A lost opportunity for that executive position.

Beware other vocal tics that reflect negatively on you: Speaking too rapidly conveys nervousness. Speaking too slowly says, "I'm a slow thinker." A volume that's excessively soft says, "I'm either bored, tired, or shy." A volume that's excessively loud says, "I'm aggressive, angry, or defiant."

Your voice—inflection, tone, intensity, pacing, pausing, volume— can be a powerful tool to control a conversation, command a crowd, communicate a culture, and ultimately create a career.

8

....

Say the Right Thing
at the Right Time
and Leave Unsaid
the Wrong Thing at
the Emotional Moment

....

The best time to hold your tongue is the time
you feel you must say something or bust.
—JOSH BILLINGS

D o you remember the days when you ran to grab the phone
on the first ring? Your parents could hardly get you to hang
up long enough to eat a meal? You clung to that curled cord as if
it were an umbilical cord tying you to your friends. Their voices
connected you to the outside world—conversations centered on
who was dating whom, who flunked what class, who hated whose
guts that week. Being grounded from the phone for an infraction
of the house rules felt like a death sentence.

Then with the advent of email, romance moved online. And
those emotional personal and business moments came through in
email "flames." Consultants warned us to let those missives cool off
before hitting the Send button. Otherwise, an email written in an

emotional moment might cost our job. They warned that the meaning got muddled in an email because the tone sounded different when delivered by text rather than tongue. What could be said with a smile and a pat on the back might not come across the same way with an exclamation point or an emoticon.

Then flaming email morphed into Facebook posts, text messages, and tweets. Shorter and more frequent became more direct and aggressive.

Only when there's a major communication foul-up that forces a manager to say, "Please pick up the phone and CALL Joe to clear up the mess" do some people realize the expedience and effectiveness of an actual conversation to clear up a problem. Recently, on a TV talk show the host probed a guest about a lawsuit regarding Medicare fraud. He asked why the victim had not called the agent earlier to report the discrepancy in the billings from the hospital and those shown on the insurance forms.

"Did you think of *calling* to report the discrepancy?" the talk-show host pressed the angry guest.

"I emailed them about it, but never got an explanation," the guest responded.

"But if what you say is true, why didn't you CALL?" the talk-show host pursued.

"Call? I didn't want to be rude!"

"Rude? You considered calling 'rude'?"

"Yes. I think calling someone today is an intrusion."

So what's at the foundation of that feeling? What would make a victim file a lawsuit before engaging in an emotional conversation?

We at Booher began to get calls several years ago from executives saying, "Our employees can't carry on a conversation any longer. They've been sitting behind a computer so long that they have difficulty talking face-to-face."

A multi-billion-dollar high-tech firm stated the problem this way: "When we have consultants on site to do a project, occasionally an executive at the client site will walk by and ask how things are going. That's a great opportunity for our consultants to tell the CEO what we've accomplished for them and mention ideas for add-on projects or to solicit their help on a stalled project. But our consultants just freeze. They can't carry on a simple conversation to engage an executive along those lines. Either they offend by complaining about the client's staff. Or they just go goofy or silent because they're talking to the CEO."

> Saying the right thing at the appropriate moment takes presence of mind and control of emotions.

But there's a bigger issue than brain-freeze when talking to C-suite executives. In many cases, people find email and texting easier than a difficult face-to-face discussion. When communicating in real time without a buffer, emotions erupt far too often. Saying the right thing at the appropriate moment takes presence of mind and control of emotions.

Make Mind Over Emotions More Than a Motto

World-renowned psychologist Paul Ekman, in his classic book *Emotions Revealed*, talks about the usefulness of auto-appraisers with his illustration of near-miss auto accidents.[14] For example, if you're driving down the freeway and see a car approaching head-on from the exit ramp, you immediately jerk the steering wheel out of the path of the oncoming car. Fear causes you to take those immediate actions without having to think to do so. Your heart starts to pump; blood races to your leg muscles; you begin to sweat. Your brain goes on automatic pilot from the emotion of fear stored in your emotional database to deliver these physical reactions.

Another example: Let's say that you grew up with an overprotective big sister telling you what to do. Twenty years later you work for a female boss. She warns you that taking a "promotion" the higher-ups have offered you in a new division will become a dead-end job within a year, with no further chance for advancement. You react angrily to your boss for trying to "control" you and accept the new job offer without investigating. Your auto-appraiser takes over from the stored emotion of anger at being "overprotected" by your "big sister" (boss).

In the case of the near-miss auto accident, these unconscious reactions can save your life. But this same unconscious reaction can cost you respect—or even your job—in other situations.

For example, let's say that colleague Joe makes an unthinking remark that embarrasses you during a meeting. You know the boss heard it. Your auto-appraiser takes over. You react out of your stored emotional database of fear. Problem? Joe's remark was simply carelessly worded; he had no intention of ill will. Others didn't take the remark seriously. But your emotions short-circuited to the emotional fear reaction. You look foolish for your inappropriate display of anger.

Analyze the link between stored past emotions and your reactions to current situations and people. Carlos, an acquaintance of mine doing an assessment for a power company, interviewed a lineman about a grievance he'd filed against the company. Even the reflective sunglasses the lineman wore could not hide his anger as he recounted with great upset the injustice done to him by management. Carlos listened for quite some time and finally stopped the lineman to ask, "When did this incident happen?"

"Fifteen years ago."

A frequent situation. A dad argues with the referee over a strikeout after his child has long forgotten the play. In reality, the argument stems from a defeat in the dad's past or a wish to relive his own childhood. A mom, feeling her own disappointment two decades earlier, takes the school principal to task because her daughter has failing grades and doesn't get to try out for cheerleader. A board member for a nonprofit charity rejects the budget recommendations because funding will not cover research for a spouse's debilitating illness. All are emotion-driven reactions.

Understanding these past links to current emotional reactions becomes a first step toward adjustment.

Moderate Your Emotions to Fit the Situation

People with presence demonstrate emotional maturity. They moderate their reactions to fit the situation, a relationship, and their goals.

People long for passionate leaders, who inspire, motivate, and engage them. But others' unbridled negative emotion feels dangerous and downright scary. That's why you sometimes feel rather helpless and even embarrassed when a colleague breaks down and cries in front of you over some disappointment like a romantic breakup or bonus that didn't come through. Out-of-control emotions feel unpredictable and put everyone "on edge."

Case in point: When I arrived on the Naval base in Maryland and first met Brad, the senior-ranking person there, he was not my idea of a military officer for several reasons. For starters, he arrived late to our 8:00 a.m. training session. Overhearing the wisecracks and "Brad" jokes, his administrative assistant spoke up to say she'd handled the "Brad problem" by telling him the start time was 7:30.

Neither was tact part of the boss's repertoire. When I posed a question for discussion, participants responded with opinions. When Brad didn't agree with them, he had no reservations in letting them know it. After all, he was the boss and obviously didn't want them to forget that. But I'll have to give him A-plus for participation. The training session was his idea. His budget was covering the cost; his team would be the benefactors if his staff learned to write better proposals and get their projects funded. So he "got with the program," and at the end of day one, he told me the customized session was right on target.

Ditto for day two. On day three, he took the entire team to lunch at a nice restaurant. But half an hour later when the workshop resumed, I posed a question to the group about outside resources for their proposals.

All of a sudden, a loud crash from the back of the room startles everyone. Everybody in the room cranes their neck toward the back to see what table or chair has crashed to the floor.

Everything still seems to be standing. The only person not stretching around to see what has happened is Brad. He sits with arms folded across his chest and eyes glaring. The query on everyone's face: "What was that?"

Had he been leaning his chair back on two legs and accidentally fallen forward with a big thud? He offers no explanation, just
sits staring toward the front. Maybe he's embarrassed, I tell myself.
So I continue the discussion. I repeat the prior question to the
group and pause for someone to offer an opinion.

All of a sudden, Brad thunders up the classroom aisle, passes
me as he exits the room, and slams the door so loudly that it rattles
the large picture hanging nearby. I turn back to the group, with a
"What's up?" expression on my face.

Some of his staff members look red-faced; others, ashen. I get
the distinct feeling that this is not the first time they'd seen that
temper. But what had set him off?

We ignore the metaphorical elephant in the room and continue our discussion of how they might revamp their proposal
templates. About forty-five minutes later, Brad saunters back into
the room as if nothing has happened, takes a seat, and participates
for the rest of the afternoon. (Later, I discovered from my colleague sitting in the back of the room that the first loud crash had
been Brad picking up his heavy three-inch workbook binder, lifting it over his head, and slamming it onto the floor.)

At the end of the workshop after all his staff had left the room,
and I was about to leave the building, Brad offered this explanation: "I want to apologize about losing my temper this afternoon.
But that just ticked me off—hearing Wendy say that we could get
outside resources to develop our proposals. That just sets up false
expectations for the others. We're never going to get approval on
outside resources. She might as well get that out of her head. I
don't want the rest of my people even hearing that crap. I know
this doesn't have anything to do with you—it's an internal problem. But she knows better than to bring up something like that.
Anyway, just an explanation. Good job today."

And he walked off.

About a month after Brad emailed to say that he and his staff
felt the workshops were very beneficial to them, our business
development manager contacted him about scheduling an additional workshop. Here was Brad's response:

Vernon,

Thanks for the email. At the present, I can't get additional funding. You're going to have to follow up with others in the organization to see about scheduling other workshops.

Happy holidays!
Brad

Six months later, Vernon emailed him an article from the *Investor's Business Daily* mentioning business communication issues that he thought might be of interest. Brad responded this way:

Vernon,

I asked you last time politely NOT to send me any more emails ever!

Brad

As Vernon showed me the two emails, he recalled an earlier comment Brad had made during a phone conversation while they were coordinating one of the earlier workshops. "I'm outta here as soon as I can find another opportunity. I'm tired of fighting the battles."

Something tells me that he's going to be "fighting the battles" wherever he goes.

A display of anger—sharp words, a splash of profanity, a slammed door, clicked heels and a sudden exit from a meeting—signals emotions out of control. A dangerous thing for the owner of such emotions—whether in person or in writing—and a scary sight for the witnesses.

Why are such emotional outbursts dangerous? In part, because they often lead to words and actions that go against our better judgment and better self—from words, to actions, and even to violence.

Like the measles, emotions are contagious. If you don't

> Like the measles, emotions are contagious. . . . Just like a cold, negative emotions need to be contained.

believe it, watch an angry mob. I dare you to attend a passionate political rally or controversial PTA meeting and come away unaffected. Just like a bad cold, negative emotions need to be contained. Likewise, sales professionals know that happy emotions expressed through smiling and nodding at buyers affect a prospect's chance of mirroring that same emotion and buying.[15]

Emotions spread. When yours erupt, they affect other people—either positively or negatively. As a result, their mirrored emotion determines others' perceptions of you.

Don't Gush

Recently, I heard a speaker reintroduce herself from the platform to a group after an absence from the industry of more than twenty years. Then during the five-minute talk, she ended with, "I love each and every one of you."

Really? Sincerely, she does? When I hear a cliché such as this (How could she? She doesn't even know them), I doubt and discount everything else that comes out of the speaker's mouth. Although the speaker is choked up at the moment, emotion will eventually give way to reason, and the speaker will be left facing a roomful of skeptics.

Even happy emotions can be out of control. Say what's sincere, then stop.

In addition to insincerity, gushing emotions suggest imma-

> Even happy emotions can be out of control. Say what's sincere, then stop.

turity. I often get emails that sound like, "Mommy! Mommy! Look! Look! There's a big red fire engine! ☺ Come see! You'll love it, too!???"

Beware the overuse of exclamation marks and emoticons that make you sound like a second-grader at the seashore. Such unbridled emotion may work well for tweets and Facebook posts, but you'll want to tone it down for more formal communication.

Choose the Way You Feel

Adopting the personality of a duffle bag doesn't cut it either. Appearing unemotional or overcontrolled is just as bad as being out of control. The goal is to choose the way you feel and how to express your emotions constructively.

How? Choose your attitude.

Body language researchers tell us that seven emotions have a universal and distinct facial expression: anger, sadness, fear, surprise, disgust, contempt, and happiness.[16] Think how many times people feel these emotions at work. Leakage happens. That is, what people feel seeps out through their body language—no matter how hard they may try to conceal it. As mentioned earlier, liars can often be detected by emotions that flicker across the face in milliseconds. That's why when people feel emotional, their voice grows husky; we say they "get all choked up." Typically, it takes a professional actor to fake an emotion—its presence or its absence.

So as not to reveal deep-seated anger, resentment, arrogance, and the like, you have to change those attitudes. Psychologist Carol Tavris, author of *Anger: The Misunderstood Emotion*, points out the dangers of expressing anger, contradicting what many amateur coaches and consultants often advise when they suggest "venting" is good for you.[17] Here are just a few of the dangers she mentions:

- Expressed anger destroys relationships.
- Angry people are socially unattractive and not well-liked.
- Expressed anger typically results in retaliation.

The goal, of course, is not to repress anger, but to rid yourself of the feeling by discovering its source and then changing the attitude and ultimately the emotion about that cause. Learn instead to talk about conflicts in a constructive way. For suggestions on how

· · · · · · · · · · · · · · · · ·

Apologies do not repair the damage done by displays of anger or arrogance. . . . Beware the perception that you show up and blow up.

· · · · · · · · · · · · · · · · ·

to deal with the five primary causes of conflict, how to mediate conflict between friends or colleagues, and how to respond to insults or criticism, you can find several hundred tips in my earlier book *Communicate with Confidence: How to Say It Right the First Time and Every Time.*

Apologies do not repair the damage done by displays of anger or arrogance. Better to choose how to express emotion appropriately than to stifle it, hoping others won't notice. They will. Beware the perception that you show up and blow up.

Emotions running amok can muck up your relationships and your reputation. Personal presence means moderating your emotional reactions so that you choose when and how to best express them.

9

Abandon Chicken Little, But Stop Sugarcoating

There is no greater impediment to the advancement of knowledge than the ambiguity of words.
—THOMAS REID

Do you remember the fable of *Chicken Little*? Just in case you've forgotten this classic, let me refresh you: One day, Chicken Little is walking in the woods when an acorn falls on her head. "Oh, my goodness!" she says, "The sky is falling! I must go tell the king." On the way to the palace, she meets Henny Penny going into the woods to hunt for berries. "Oh no, don't go!" she says, "I was just there, and the sky was falling! Come with me to tell the king." So Henny Penny follows her.

They follow along until they meet Cocky Locky, who was going into the woods to hunt for seeds. "Oh no, don't go!" says Chicken Little. "I was just there, and the sky was falling! Come with me to tell the king." So Cocky Locky follows her and Henny Penny.

They follow along until they meet Turkey Lurkey going into the woods to look for berries. Same drill.

Finally, they meet up with Foxy Woxy, who asks where they're going. Same warning from the feathered friends. But instead of following Chicken Little, Foxy Woxy says, "I know a shortcut to the palace." Rather than the palace, he leads them to the entrance

• • • • • • • • • • • • • • •

Presence stems from perception. People shy away from those who jump to conclusions without checking the facts and worry rather than weigh options.

• • • • • • • • • • • • • • •

of the foxhole, where he plans to gobble them for dinner.

Just as they are about to enter, the king's hunting dogs rush up growling and howling. They chase the fox away and save Chicken Little and her other fine-feathered friends. The smart king gives her an umbrella to carry for future walks in the woods.

So what's the moral of this fable where personal presence is concerned? Consider the credibility gap the next time Chicken Little warns colleagues about impending danger.

Ask George W. Bush how he felt when the Coalition forces discovered no WMDs in Iraq. Never mind that the rest of the world thought Saddam Hussein had WMDs hidden there as well. Never mind that members of Congress from both parties also thought they'd find WMDs there. The former president writes in his memoir *Decision Points*, "No one was more shocked and angry than I was when we didn't find the weapons. . . . I had a sickening feeling every time I thought about it. I still do." In various interviews during his book tour, the former president explained that his disappointment stemmed from the fear about the change in perception of the war in the minds of the America people and their support of the effort to rid the world of Saddam and free the Iraqi people.[18]

Presence stems from perception. The president understood the critical importance of perception in leadership, decision making, and decisive action.

People shy away from those who jump to conclusions without checking the facts and who worry rather than weigh options. Worry leads to a gloom-and-doom demeanor, poor judgment, and hasty overreactions.

Nor are people attracted to those who practice hand-wringing and preach doom and gloom. A message of despair goes against human nature and the need to hope for the best. Who gets up in the morning and says, "I think I'll turn on the news. Sure hope we had a terrorist attack somewhere last night. Or maybe a tornado or tsunami came through, knocked down some buildings, and killed someone I know"? Know anybody who buys a lottery ticket and tells the cashier, "Well, I'm betting this is a losing number"? Ever have a teammate say to you, "When this project was assigned to us, I was hoping it was going to be more difficult than what the boss described"?

People with presence think positively and want to be around others who do the same. Mature optimism is a cornerstone of healthy living. So when you're habitually complaining that "the sky is falling," they draw the conclusion that you're overwhelmed, unprepared, and incapable of dealing with situations. None of which leads to building your presence and credibility.

That said, people don't subscribe to the Emperor-Has-No-Clothes philosophy either. When a serious situation develops, leaders do not resort to pep talks and platitudes, pretending that all is well and that there's nothing to be concerned about when everyone involved knows differently.

Leaders know that words shape thought. They provide healthy diets of hope while acknowledging a negative situation. All change—personal or organizational—begins by seeing reality and then creating a vision to improve upon it.

Acknowledge the Truth

If sales are sinking, say so. If your team is performing poorly, own up to the numbers. If the organization looks lousy beside the competition, come clean about the market feedback. Nothing opens people's minds and raises their estimation of your credibility like admitting the truth—and nothing decreases your credibility like ignoring the obvious or blaming, demonizing, or scapegoating others. You understand how pathetic it looks if you've ever heard politicians try to explain away election results after a dramatic loss or listened to CEOs try to explain away poor earnings after failure to achieve their goals.

Almost weekly, CEOs are asked to respond during media interviews about their organizations' financial health. A few find it difficult to acknowledge the facts. You may recall this statement from Richard Fuld, former CEO of Lehman Brothers: "We are on the right track to put these last two quarters behind us." Five days later, Lehman's declared bankruptcy, the largest in U.S. history.

Lesson two: Accept responsibility for any part of the problem or situation you caused. Small people run from responsibility. Strong people shoulder it.

> **Small people run from responsibility. Strong people shoulder it.**

Stop Sugarcoating the Unknown and Unknowable

"You'll do fine!" "Everything's going to be fine—just wait and see." "It'll all work itself out. It always does." Such are the assurances parents give their kids. You expect them and even appreciate them—at age thirteen. But to an adult hearing such platitudes from bosses, colleagues, or friends who could not possibly know the future and how a situation will actually turn out, the remarks sound empty, if not insulting to our intelligence.

That's not to say you can't offer comforting words. You can and should. But to be helpful and consoling, they should be the *right* words. People with presence know what to say when a colleague, friend, or family member experiences the death of a loved one, divorce, job loss, difficulty with a parent or child, or other tragedy or loss that produces strong emotion. Entire books have been written on these topics. (For my guidelines on what to say or write in these circumstances, go to www.sympathylettersonline.com.)

People with presence strive to get past the clichés and all-will-be-well platitudes to meaningful comments that comfort and help. They make an effort and care enough to learn to say the right thing at the right time.

Leaders understand the apprehension others feel about a potentially negative situation, and they can acknowledge that they don't have all the answers. Most important, they feel powerful enough to sustain people with their presence rather than empty promises.

Focus on Options

In a negative situation, people with presence focus others on positive alternatives and actions with the power of their words.

Several years back, I was a member of a large megachurch where an audit revealed that the pastor and a few staff members had misused funds, leaving the congregation on the verge of bankruptcy, with a more than $6.2 million debt. As a result of that situation, I had occasion to watch the lay leadership team there be straightforward about the reality of the situation, yet focus on positive alternatives and actions.

By their inspiring words, prayer, and a positive plan of action, within three years the church had paid off the massive debt incurred by the impropriety and had accumulated surplus funds. In fact, the lay leaders and new church staff led members to found another nonprofit with the excess funds collected: 6 Stones Mission Network. Now a separate and self-sustaining nonprofit, 6 Stones (www.6stones.org) offers a plethora of services to surrounding communities: rebuilding houses condemned by the city governments, providing free food and clothing to the needy, offering medical and educational assistance, and providing counseling services.

This nonprofit has received the following awards for their work in the Dallas–Fort Worth Metroplex: Community Service Award from the Chamber of Commerce, Volunteer Organization of the Year from the tri-city school district, and Volunteer Organization of the Year from the City of Euless, Texas.

What could have been an emotional, spiritual, financial, and legal disaster for its almost 10,000 members and their families has become an inspiration and a lifeline to literally thousands more.

To increase your credibility, stop sugarcoating, but ditch the down-in-the-mouth demeanor. Become a thought leader with helpful straight talk about the substantive issues.

10

. . . .

Move the Conversation Forward

. . . .

Your conversation is your advertisement.
Every time you open your mouth
you let men look into your mind.
—BRUCE BURTON

Typically when journalists call for an interview, they have a story angle in mind with questions prepared to lead the interview. But often their questions don't really get at the heart of the matter. That's not their fault, of course. It's just that they don't know the topic as well as the person being interviewed. So if a subject-matter expert simply responds to the questions, many reporters hang up the phone either disappointed or without the whole story.

Enter the concept of "talking points"—media training 101 for authors, movie stars, politicians, CEOs, and anyone who's going to be in the public eye. Others who want to elevate their presence in the marketplace can pick up a tip or two about this concept.

Prepare Talking Points

Have you ever tried to engage someone in conversation when you get only limited responses? Imagine yourself in the following exchange:

"Depak and Sonya host great get-togethers, don't they?" you toss out.

"Yes, they do."

Silence.

You try again: "I hear the Engineering team got turned down on their patent application last week. I guess that was a big disappointment. They had been counting on that to launch an entire line of engines."

"That's what I hear."

Silence.

"How will that affect your department?" you persist.

"I don't know yet."

Even an automated greeting responds well enough to take you to the next menu option.

When you know you'll be participating in an important meeting discussion, giving an opinion on a controversial issue, or defending a budget increase, prepare ahead of time a list of key points you want to communicate. How many and how detailed? There's no set rule. But two is too few, and nine is too many. Just be clear, be brief, and be memorable.

Here's an example of my talking points for one short interview on my earlier book *The Voice of Authority: 10 Communication Strategies Every Leader Needs to Know*:

Information is not communication.

Information is to communication what X-rays are to surgery.

— Current: Be responsive.

— Consistent: Words vs. policies

— Concerned: Hospital surveys

These five memory joggers can carry me through a five-minute or a forty-five-minute interview. They form the skeleton upon which hang the muscle of my ideas and elaboration.

Whatever your important meeting, conversation, networking agenda, or setting, prepare talking points rather than scramble through to the finish line.

Learn to Bridge

You've seen those "You Are Here" maps in malls or amusement parks. Consider bridging statements those that move the conversation or meeting from where it is to where you want to go. The goal: Simply decide on the appropriate linking phrase that leads from the present topic to your entry point. Here are some of the more generic bridging statements that will almost always serve you well:

— "One of the *more critical questions* we need to ask ourselves regarding this situation is blah, blah, blah . . ."
— "I think the *more urgent* issue is . . ."
— "Actually, *what excites me most* about this entire project is . . ."
— "Let's not forget that the *key to our success* here will be . . ."
— "What we don't want to overlook in all these details is the *overriding goal* of . . ."
— "You may be right about all the considerations mentioned, but to me *the real value* will be in . . ."
— "That's all true, but let's not forget the *fundamental flaw* in this plan is . . ."
— "While all these details are intriguing, the *central issue* is still . . ."
— "I understand your point. The *crucial test* of the plan, however, will be . . ."
— "These things aside, our *real concern* must always be . . ."

Such bridging statements lead to the next intersection of ideas. They focus discussion and help mark you as a thought leader.

Reframe to Action

Parents do it. Spouses do it. Salespeople do it. Lawmakers do it. Politicians do it. Governments do it. They all reframe ideas to help reshape how people think.

You: "So why can't I go to the party? Everybody else's parents are letting them go!"

Your parent: "So if everybody else jumped off a building, would you want to jump too?"

If you had this conversation with a parent growing up, raise your hand. That's reframing a situation as a parent. We've been exposed to it since birth by everyone who wants to influence us.

When older job seekers fear a potential employer might hesitate to hire because of age, they reframe answers by emphasizing experience. I recall interviewing an older applicant, Suzanne, who wanted twice the salary of recent graduates in the field. When I asked about why the salary differential over her competitors, she reframed this way: "What I bring to the table over some of the more recent graduates is maturity and judgment that you'll not find in a thirty-year-old." Then she went on to tick off all the decisions that required mature judgment in the job.

Another successful reframing on the same age issue: Ronald Reagan in 1984. Many feared that he could not defeat Walter Mondale because of his advancing age, and Reagan was looking for opportunity to put the issue to rest. When the question of age came up in the debate, he responded with this reframe of the age question: "I will not make age an issue of this campaign. I am not going to exploit, for political purposes, my opponent's youth and inexperience." Reagan's one-liner brought down the house. Even Mondale laughed. And the age issue disappeared from campaign discussions.

But reframing happens in everyday situations with far less effort, even with subtle word choices: " Layoffs" are now about "rightsizing." A "used car" is now a "pre-owned car." "Salespeople" are now "advisors" and "consultants." "Tax cuts" are now "tax relief." The "private schools" debate is now about "school choice." Organizations no longer have "problems"; they have only "challenges" or "initiatives." People no longer "disagree" with their colleagues; they simply have "issues" with their colleagues' opinions.

And, of course, politicians will continue to use reframing to lead voters to the polls. Abortion has been reframed as a "pro-choice" matter. When the healthcare bill was introduced, its "review boards" were reframed as "death panels." To clients, sales professionals reframe "cost" as "investment." Learning from them, politicians have reframed our "deficit spending" and "debt" as "investment in the future."

Reframing occurs on a larger scale with situations such as these:

— A voter says, "I disagree with the mayor's policy." The mayor or her supporters reframe the opposition like this: "People have always had racial biases in our community, but we intend to carry forth this policy regardless of those who stand against me." (The opposition is framed as racial prejudice rather than policy disagreement.)

— A parent protests on-campus activities at his child's school, but the school board refuses to vote in his favor on the issue. The parent reframes the vote in his letter to the editor of the local newspaper: "Members of the school board refused to ban this group on-campus activity because they fear reaction from a small gang of popular students and their parents." (The opposition is framed as favoritism toward a vocal minority rather than a difference over school policy.)

These reframes represent selfish or otherwise negative reasons.

But if you want to be considered a thought leader, look for situations where there's discord and reframe to bring people together. Rather than permitting reframing to create conflict and deception, call attention to illogical thinking and bring issues to clarity.

Look for potentially negative situations and reframe them positively to lead people to accept change. Look for colleagues who are either displeased with their career advancement or who feel stuck in a no-win situation, and reframe opportunities to help them develop their full potential. They'll look to you as a catalyst for action and possibly as their mentor.

Several years ago in our own organization, we hired someone from a large financial institution as our vice president of marketing. A warm and personable individual, she quickly connected with her support team as they set about to establish new strategic marketing initiatives with the ultimate goal for her to assume the role of general manager. But after several months, it became apparent that she lacked the background for that ultimate goal and we decided to part ways. After I announced the resignation to the staff, her direct support staff person was disappointed by her departure, fearing that their plans during the past six months would not come to fruition. In her eyes, all was lost with her boss's departure.

But another marketing specialist in the same job function reframed the situation to her friend this way: "This gives us an opportunity to show what we can do ourselves. We've had a big part in putting these plans together. Really, all she did was lead the meetings and have us brainstorm ideas. You and I always executed the plans anyway."

That reframing was all it took to change her friend's thinking. Both staffers executed the plans as designed.

It's the classic glass-half-empty or glass-half-full situation that you influence by your words. Reframing typically reshapes the thought process with my coaching clients. Some bosses, who often initiate the coaching process, haven't done a good job in explaining why they're sending someone for coaching. So the individual to be coached arrives with this attitude: "My performance must be unsatisfactory. If I don't do better, they may pass me over for promotion. My job may even be in jeopardy."

But with other clients, the CEO has done an excellent job of explaining why he or she would like the individual to have coaching. Those clients arrive at our training center excited about the sessions. Usually within our first couple of hours together, they'll share a previous conversation with their boss, which typically goes something like this recent one: "I report to our CFO, who's very good on his feet. I've attended our annual shareholders meetings and also the all-hands meeting with about 2,800 of us in the financial area. He keeps his cool, no matter how they grill him. He says he's had these coaching sessions with you himself and that it's been very valuable for him. So I feel fortunate that the company's spending this kind of money on me. I want to make the most of our time together."

Reframing makes all the difference.

Reframe to reshape thinking toward commitment rather than complaint, toward solutions rather than problems, toward action rather than inaction.

Just as in sports, most any player on the field can catch the conversational ball and fall with it—either fumble it or recover it. But the stars catch the ball and carry it forward. People with presence get their message across, either by reframing or bridging to their talking points.

When someone tosses you a conversational pass, play to score.

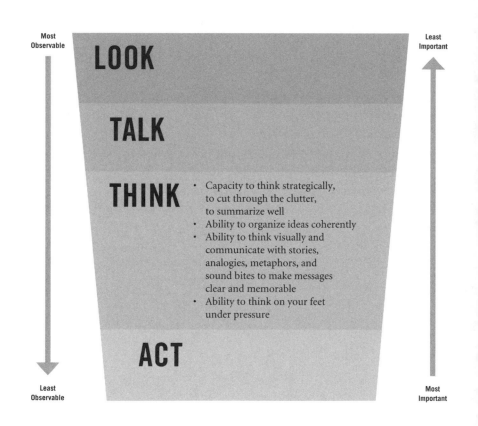

Most
Observable

LOOK

TALK

THINK
- Capacity to think strategically, to cut through the clutter, to summarize well
- Ability to organize ideas coherently
- Ability to think visually and communicate with stories, analogies, metaphors, and sound bites to make messages clear and memorable
- Ability to think on your feet under pressure

ACT

Least
Important

Least
Observable

Most
Important

PART 3: HOW YOU THINK

11

....

Think Strategically

....

I like thinking big. I always have.
If you're going to be thinking anyway,
you might as well think big.
—DONALD TRUMP

S trategic thinking sets you apart from the crowd. So what is strategic thinking versus tactical thinking and how does it set you
apart as a person with presence? First, consider these differences:

Strategic Thinking Vs. Tactical Thinking

Central common vision or organizing statement **vs.**
Day-to-day actions or operations

Long-term concern **vs.** Short-term concern

Understanding why to do something **vs.**
Understanding how to do something

Mental, conceptual **vs.** Physical, tangible

Doing the right thing **vs.** Doing things right

Focused **vs.** Scattered, many "balls in the air"

Roadmaps **vs.** Tools for the trip

Structure **vs.** Who and what gets placed into the structure

---

- - - - - - - - - - - - - - - -

The person with presence knows the why behind the what and the how.

- - - - - - - - - - - - - - - - -

The most significant of these differences has to be the central organizing statement: What's the goal, purpose, message, lesson learned, conclusion, or plan? The person with presence knows the why behind the what and how.

Sort the Significant from the Trivial

Once you understand the overriding principle of why, other things from the previous chart fall into place: Doing the right thing. Focusing. Creating the road map. Sorting and sifting become second nature in your day-to-day tasks.

Giving evidence of your ability to think strategically, you select appropriate information to pass on to others and forego the urge to hit the "Send" button every time new stats hit your inbox. Squelch the urge to "speak your truth" in a meeting every time a thought flitters across your brain.

One of the most frequent difficulties among coaching clients is concern about preparing strategic presentations at the appropriate level for the boardroom. They typically express it as Roger did not long ago: "I give this typical briefing monthly in an all-hands meeting, then quarterly to the president of our business unit. Once a year I fly to headquarters and deliver it at Corporate. I'm just not sure about how detailed to get. Our president has told me several times that I need to stay out of the weeds." He shrugged. "But I'm an engineer."

Roger's self-assessment proved accurate. His boss had phoned me before our session to pass on his assessment. "Roger's a brilliant guy. But he needs a little polish before he moves to the executive suite. He gets far too detailed in his presentations. In fact, he gets lost—particularly during the Q&A. He knows so much about the subject that he wants to tell them *everything* and he's indecisive about *what* to tell them. As a consequence, he sounds like a bumbling fool." His suggestion for my time with Roger: Help him learn to sort the tactical from the strategic and the trivial from the significant in his presentations.

During the president's next televised address to the country regarding financial reform, can you imagine hearing him explain how to complete a 1040 tax form? Or what if the Secretary of Defense attempted to tell you which military units in which countries had been trained on which weapons? Would they have trouble maintaining your interest?

Instead, the president lays out his strategy regarding taxation: Taxes are either going up or down on this or that group of people. The Secretary of Defense tells us that we have a growing threat from the terrorists in a certain country and that we're tightening security measures there by not accepting shipments from that country. They have a strategic message to deliver and refuse to get sidetracked on tactical details.

(Before you argue that you know too many people who have their heads so far in the clouds that they're no earthly good, let me clarify what I mean about the significant versus the trivial: A toothache can be significant if it happens to be *your* tooth and you're drugged on painkillers the day you're speaking to Wall Street analysts.)

Know how to sift the significant from the myriad data you have at hand. Your reputation rests on what you choose to say, how you allocate your time, and what information you decide to distribute.

> Know how to sift the significant from the myriad data you have at hand. Your reputation rests on what you choose to say, how you allocate your time, and what information you decide to distribute.

Adjust Your Zoom Lens

Dr. Rosabeth Moss Kanter, professor of business administration at Harvard University, suggests an apt metaphor for two modes of strategic thinking: Consider the zoom lens on a camera. You can zoom in and get a close look at specific details—but be so close that you miss the bigger context and can't make sense of what you're seeing. Zoom out and see the big picture—but you may miss key details and subtleties that would prevent a bad decision. In her *Harvard Business Review* article, Dr. Kanter points out the virtues and drawbacks of both perspectives for leaders.[19]

Like a camera with a malfunctioning zoom lens, some people get stuck in one mode of strategic thinking. That mode may be strategic in many ways, but still limiting. Take a manager I'll call Kelly Smith as an example. As an entrepreneur, Kelly launches a new advertising agency. As the firm grows, she may plow all her profit back into the business, open up new agencies in new cities as soon as she can afford to do so, and rent prestigious office space in those cities as soon as she lands a couple of key corporate clients to pay the overhead and salaries in those firms. She may get carried away with the allure of growing revenue, building a "national" reputation, and creating an impressive client list.

But four years into the venture, she finds herself working eighteen-hour days and emotionally spent, with no systems in place, no professional management team in place, all clients calling her for "special" deals because she's the one who brought them on board, and short on cash flow to complete the next project. Kelly may be strategic in her vision and quick to take advantage of opportunities, but she "zooms in" too often on specifics to see the overall financial and staffing landscape.

After Kelly wears herself out, let's say she takes a long sabbatical and then returns to work determined to zoom out. What happens if she gets stuck there? She may fail to see and deal with rising frustration of her employees in the various cities. She may not see emerging trends in the advertising industry, may miss a key opportunity to buy out a competitor in Peoria, may be blind to an innovative technology that clients are asking about. Operating above the fray, she may be leaning on strategies, principles, and processes that have outlived their time in a fast-paced industry.

If you've ever hired a professional photographer for an important occasion—like a wedding, family reunion, graduation, parents' fiftieth wedding anniversary cruise—then you know they'll shoot hundreds of photos to end up with forty to fifty usable ones. Close-ups catch the emotion, excitement, and energy. Wide shots capture the context and relationships. You savor both.

So people with presence can't let themselves get stuck with only one view available—even if strategic. They keep adjusting the lens to see the facts, situation, problem, or decision from all vantage points. Then they decide and take action.

Ask "Why Not?"

You may not be leading the free world, but every leader can think strategically about his or her job or projects. Although there's no commonly accepted definition of strategic thinking, recent thought says strategic thinking focuses on the "why" and "what if" (not the "what" of conventional thinking). Why do things a certain way? How might we get different, better results? How can we take advantage of opportunities before us?

Why not go one step further to focus on the "why not"? Look at what others are doing and focus in the opposite direction. Why not do things differently? I'm not talking about being a contrarian just for the sake of attention—just for branding purposes—but to generate thinking about streamlined processes, take advantage of new opportunities, and raise provocative product ideas.

When reporting on a problem, the tactical thinker will tell how he corrected a current situation or what is wrong with your vision, idea, or plan. The strategic thinker will tell how she will circumvent the problem altogether or take advantage of opportunities the "problem" created. The book *Flash Foresight*, by my colleague and entrepreneur Dan Burrus, outlines seven strategic thinking principles for doing just that:[20]

- Start with certainty about hard trends.
- Anticipate. Base strategies on what you know about the future.
- Transform. Use technology-driven change to your advantage.
- Take your biggest problem and skip it. Find the real problem.
- Go opposite. Do what no one else is doing.
- Redefine and reinvent. Leverage your uniqueness.
- Direct your future.

The best of these is his principle "Going Opposite." Every time Dan and I have chatted about our work and answer the typical "What's new with you?" question, he always sings the same refrain, "I try to find out what everybody else is doing—and not do that." His book presents a plethora of examples to prove how well the principle works: Southwest Airlines, Amazon, Crocs, JetBlue, Netflix, Starbucks, Zappos.

> People with presence rarely rush to judgment—of people, situations, data. They make it a practice to listen first, to observe, to collect and assess information.

Practice Intake Before Output

People with presence rarely rush to judgment—of people, situations, data. They make it a practice to listen first, to observe, to collect and assess information. As a member of two CEO forum groups and also in my consulting work, I'm continually reminded of this differentiator: People with a strong presence stay alert, take in information, and think before they speak. Those who lack presence are short on the intake, quick to speak their mind, and often regret their output.

Ask Thought-Provoking Questions of Others

Executive management teams insist that a key value advisory boards offer is asking the right questions to guide thinking and prevent missteps. Effective consultants provide their clients the same service. They go into an organization, listen to the situation and plans, analyze data, and ask questions. Their value most often lies not in the answers they provide but in the questions they ask.

Inventors stumble upon new processes and new products because they have great curiosity and continually ask others or themselves provocative questions—and then go discover or develop the answers.

Strategic thinkers through the decades have asked questions like these:

— Why do we need a person to operate this equipment? Can we automate this process?
— How could we stop providing this service to our clients and still charge the same overall fee?
— Would customers prefer to serve themselves rather than pay extra for service?
— Would people pay a premium fee for personalized service? If so, how do we personalize ours?
— Will individuals auction, buy, and sell expensive second-hand items online without examining the items firsthand?
— Why would people read novels from a screen?
— Why would people spend real dollars on an imaginary plot of ground in cyberspace?

. . . .

The more provocative your question, generally the stronger others consider your presence and your contribution to the outcome.

. . . .

Make Sure Your Writing Reflects Your Thinking

In their autobiographies, Jack Welch, former chairman and CEO of General Electric, and Lee Iacocca, legendary chairman and CEO of Chrysler, insist that one of their key reasons for asking subordinates to submit reports was to see how they think. They wanted to see how well they could make a case for this or that course of action. Could the writer see opportunities and analyze risks and rewards logically? Such reports served as their platforms or "tryouts" for promotions.

On the downside: It is possible to think strategically, but still not write well because you haven't developed your writing skills. People may hear you say something, and three days later forget how well or how poorly you expressed your ideas. When you write, however, your thinking is captured permanently for all to see. Your persona stays linked intricately to that photo of your thought process.

So consider the critical importance of excellent writing skills as a snapshot of strategic thinking.

Your presence of mind showcases your distinct way of thinking in a manner just as recognizable as your body language. You are what and how you think.

Strategic thinking uniquely positions you as the go-to person for sharp focus, sound problem analysis, and innovative ideas. My point is not that tactical thinking is unnecessary. On the contrary. Goals demand tactical execution. Tactical thinking is critical—but it's vastly more common among your colleagues. And typically, it's the strategic thinkers who sign the paychecks.

12

. . . .

Cut Through the Clutter

. . . .

If it takes a lot of words to say what you have in mind,
give it more thought.
—DENNIS ROCH

It was the best of times, it was the worst of times." That famous opening from Charles Dickens's *A Tale of Two Cities* illustrates three key principles for how people with presence think and plan their communication:

- Grab attention to be heard.
- Summarize succinctly to be clear.
- Be brief to be appreciated.

Beginnings should grab people's attention whether you're writing an epic novel, telling an anecdote, or presenting your budget for the year. But beginnings can't go on too long, or they become the muddled middle. That's why the conventional wisdom in Hollywood is that you'll never sell your movie if you can't summarize the plot in a sentence.

My twist on that in the marketplace: You'll never sell your idea in the boardroom if you can't summarize it in a paragraph. How best to get started on that goal?

"If you can't write your message in a sentence, you can't say it in an hour." That line came from my earlier book *Speak with Confidence: Powerful Presentations That Inform, Inspire, and Persuade*, and I first tweeted it in early 2009 as one of my daily tips for presenters. As I write almost two years later, that comment is still being re-tweeted. Its long life in cyberspace, I think, can be attributed to the frustration people feel in being trapped in a conversation or meeting by colleagues who ramble on and on without making a clear point.

Corporations pay ad agencies millions of dollars each year to create ads to do just that. They also pay network and cable TV millions to run Super Bowl ads with one succinct message. In fact, competition among sponsors of the Super Bowl ads has overshadowed the football game itself in some years. Who can get the point across in the fewest words possible to get the biggest laugh has become the name of the Super Bowl ad game. Granted, after-the-game analysts suggest that some ads miss the market on that first criterion: getting the point across. The ad gets a laugh and a vote—but the next day, nobody remembers the product or message.

> You'll never sell your idea in the boardroom if you can't summarize it in a paragraph.

That reality brings me to my next point: People with presence have a knack for cutting through the clutter and expressing the core message *clearly*.

You've probably heard the old joke among salespeople about their product offerings to customers: "We can deliver it to you cheap, quick, and good. Pick any two." Contrary to what some technical professionals argue is the impossible, strategic thinkers deliver their message both briefly and clearly.

Let's dig deeper into these three principles—being brief, clear, and thought-provoking.

Grab Their Attention to Be Heard

Dave Cote, CEO of Honeywell Corporation, opened a recent speech to the U.S. Chamber of Commerce this way:

The seeds of the next recession have already been planted. The debt burden accumulated over the next ten years will sink us. And a decision will get made . . . one of two ways. One way is to do it now, proactively, and thoughtfully. The second way is to wait until the bond market forces us to do it. We can ask Greece what that's like.

This presentation will start and end with the same message. That is, "Do we still have the political will to do the hard things required in life? Would we rather pull together . . . or pull apart?" It's an important question for all of us Americans. Some countries don't think America will ever be able to fix the issue because we no longer have the political will to get the tough things done, that our time is past, that we'd rather argue and blame others than take responsibility for a collectively critical decision. As an American, I disagree with that view. . . . But I also know it requires the American people to *push* and the President and the Congress to *lead* to make it happen. And *each* of you can help.

Hopefully, I have your attention . . . so let's begin.[21]

Would you agree that CFO Cote did not mince words with a warm up drill? He had their attention.

On the other hand, my client Pete seemed a bit irritated at himself during our session together. I had asked him to rethink his opening sentence for a presentation he was preparing to deliver for his upcoming session before his board of directors. He'd spent ten minutes doodling on his yellow tablet, trying to rework his thoughts before standing to practice his opening segment again.

Once again, he started with a warm-up drill: "I appreciate the time today to give you a brief overview of our successes with the four new product lines we introduced this past year, to explain the marketing challenges we've faced, and to tell you how we plan to handle those in the coming months. First, as you know, blah, blah, blah, . . ."

He continued for another two or three minutes describing what he was *going* to tell them—later—in his twenty-minute time slot.

"Pete, let me stop you here." I turned off the camera and repeated my earlier request to him. "What we need is a great opening segment that really informs them. Something that piques their interest or demonstrates marketing successes or challenges this year. Let's try the opening again with your bottom-line message right upfront—the one we developed earlier." We had already gone through the thinking stage, and he clearly had in mind the key point he wanted to make. In fact, as we chatted in casual conversation, he articulated his key message well and ticked off three sub-points to support that message. He had anecdotes and illustrations for each point. So why had he "gone blank" now that he was on his feet in front of the camera?

He started again. "Thank you for attending. . . . What I want to do is to overview blah, blah, blah. . . ." Same problem. He delivered a purpose statement—a promise to tell the audience something *later*. I stopped him a second time.

"Pete, you're still giving a purpose statement. You're promising to tell me something—later. Tell me NOW. What's the bottom line about marketing? I'm ready to go to lunch!"

He broke out in a grin, stuck his hands in his pocket, and just started to shake his head in a hangdog, schoolboy fashion. "I'm doing it again, aren't I?"

I nodded.

"I hate it when my own people do that to me. In fact, I interrupt them when they come in and start to tell me some long tale. Just like you interrupted me. I don't have time for it. I tell them to cut to the chase. And here I am, trying to do that in my own presentation to a roomful of CEO-types."

The third time was the charm. He grasped the concept. "Do unto others . . ."

Summarize Succinctly to Be Clear

Sounds simple. It rarely is.

Maybe you've seen this commercial for The Ladders, the online job site exclusively for $100K+ candidates looking for $100K+ jobs (www.theladders.com). The commercial opens with a tennis match in progress. But soon you discover the two players on the court can't return the ball to each other because people start running onto the court randomly and getting in their way—very unsuitable people, inappropriately dressed for the game, overweight and out of shape, without the proper tennis equipment, unfocused and inattentive to the game going on around them. Tennis balls bounce randomly to and fro across the net. Hundreds of would-be players slam into each other, swinging rackets and briefcases in all directions, trying to hit balls every which way.

The real players stand aside, frustrated at the chaos on the court.

In about the last ten seconds of the commercial, the voice-over says, "If you think about it, this is the trouble with most job search sites: When you let everyone play, nobody wins." The website address appears on the screen, along with the text: "The most $100K+ jobs." Fade to end.

A clear, concise summary of a problem and the solution. A classy commercial that suggests its creators understand the critical importance of cutting through the clutter to the core message.

With tweets limited to 140 characters and people texting in syllables and letters because words take too long (R U OK?), people have little patience with those who can't "say it in a sentence" and stop.

With the explosive growth of Twitter, Facebook, YouTube, and LinkedIn, information continues to bombard people. Your presence cannot be felt unless you can say or write your message succinctly.

To understand the importance of summary, consider voice-mails. Have you ever felt frustration when you have a few minutes to pick up your voicemails and you have several messages likes this: "Hey, this is B.J. Just wanted to check in with you to see how things are going. I just got in last night from Chicago. The weather was terrible, and we sat out on the runway for more than an hour before we left. But anyway, I'm now in LA and have picked up Tseuko at her hotel and we're heading for the client's site. Two things that might be a problem there that I'd like to talk to you

> If Twitter has no other benefit than helping people get their point across in 140 characters or fewer, it will have been a revolutionary exercise in a core competency.

about before we go in to make the presentation. One involves the safety issue and the other is about pricing. We're going to stop and get a bite of lunch before our meeting, but it's critical that we talk because—" Bleep, the phone cuts off.

How about emails? Do you have to read them twice, sorting and organizing the details to deduce the message because there's no clear summary that says it all?

If Twitter has no other benefit than helping people get their point across in 140 characters or fewer, it will have been a revolutionary exercise in a core competency. Notice, however, how few can do so. Summarize succinctly to cut through the clutter to the core message, problem, solution, or issue.

Be Brief to Be Appreciated

On our Booher survey, we asked participants the most common complaint they hear about presentations in their organizations. "Too long for the intended purpose" was the response from 25 percent of the survey participants. Another 20 percent reported that the message and purpose were unclear.

Conclusion: Roughly half of the survey respondents confirmed that people have difficulty getting to the point. Lengthy, disorganized presentations leave listeners wondering:

1. "What's the message?" or

2. "What do you want me to *do* about the message?" or

3. "Why did you waste so much time *giving* me that message?"

Although clearly connected, brevity and summary are not synonymous. A summary is a comprehensive restatement of main points or conclusions, a shorter version of something longer. But that "shorter version" may not be brief. In fact, some proposal "summaries" fill a three-ring binder. Some presenters deliver project "summaries" lasting an hour.

While giving a comprehensive summary has great value, a summary is not necessarily brief. Brief is better.

Lawyers understand the value of succinct summaries in the courtroom. Although lawyers can be loquacious when they're drafting a letter or contract, most practice the principles of brevity in persuasive situations—such as battling for a client's life. They address the jury with the opening bottom-line message even before witnesses take the stand: "Ladies and gentlemen of the jury, I intend to prove that my client, Darrin DoGood, is innocent of this crime. There is no motive. There are no witnesses. And on the night in question, my client was registered at a Hilton Hotel in Houston."

According to Voltaire, "The best way to be boring is to leave nothing out." The best way to be appreciated is to say your piece and shut up.

People with presence think strategically, understand the critical link between focus and clarity, and appreciate the value of time. State your case and move on.

13

Take a Point of View

*Any clod can have the facts;
having opinions is an art.*
—CHARLES MCCABE

After being hired to help an investment company develop and shape their message to potential clients, I listened to four executive vice presidents as they presented their segments of the "official" company overview. The General Counsel presented his overview of real estate investment options and the new tax laws that applied.

When he finished, I asked him, "So do you think real estate is a good investment for your high-net-worth clients?"

"Absolutely the best," he said. "For several reasons." And he listed them for me.

"Why didn't you include those reasons in your presentation?" I asked.

"I did."

"Hmmm. Well, I missed them."

"Maybe they didn't come across as reasons. But the facts were there: The full occupancy rates of the apartment buildings and the commercial properties. The low turnover. All the facts demonstrate a great return over a ten-year period. Any investor should have drawn that conclusion."

"But why would you leave it to the listener to draw that conclusion? Why not just tell them real estate is a good investment?"

"Well, I'm a lawyer. I didn't want to come across as a used car salesman!"

For the next hour, we discussed the difference between hype and persuasion.

After all, his organization spent several million dollars every year flying in estate planners, financial advisors, brokers and potential clients to persuade them to invest in real estate. Why would he not want to lead them to a conclusion?

Be clear about your purpose. If you're asked just to dump information, do it. But far more often than not, executives expect you—even need you— to take a point of view about the information you're providing them.

He couldn't give me an answer. When I later mentioned that conversation to the president of his firm, the CEO had an answer: "We do most definitely want our investor clients to leave our conference with that conclusion!"

Be clear about your purpose. If you're asked just to dump information, do it. But far more often than not, executives expect—even need—you to take a point of view about the information you're providing them.

For some reason, specialists—accountants, systems analysts, engineers, human resource specialists—resist this idea. Don't ask me why. They just do. Dave, an accountant at a large oil company, finished a feasibility study and delivered the report to the executive team. Big flop. Dave ducked out of the meeting, feeling as though he might get hit with a pink slip by the end of the week. And the worst part was that he didn't even understand why. But when he recounted the situation to me, it became clear.

The original question from the executive team was this: What's the best way to acquire this land for our new manufacturing site? Outright purchase? Capital lease? Operating lease? Installment purchase, or some other option? Dave had answered the question like a schoolboy; he'd explained all the options, along with the pros and cons of each.

"So what did you recommend they should do?" I asked him as he played ain't-it-awful with me after the executives had pounced on him.

"Well, I didn't make a recommendation. I didn't feel that was my place."

"Why not?"

"Well, I'm . . . we're . . . my team just did the study. That's all I was asked to do—to look at the possibilities."

"But you have an opinion, don't you?"

"Sure. Given the fact that they want to eventually own the land and given the new tax laws, we're going to come out ahead with an outright purchase."

"So why didn't you just recommend that upfront?"

"I didn't know it was my place."

It was his place.

Still not convinced?

Let's say you go to your attorney's office with a legal question: "I have some property in Podunk County, and the city there is trying to force me to sell some of my land for a park and state museum. Here's the letter and explanation they sent me. Can they force me to sell the land to them if I don't want to—and for this paltry price?"

Now do you want your attorney to give you an opinion about where you stand on the issue? Or do you want her just to cite various court cases and rulings from the past and let you draw your own conclusions about how similar your case might be to those past situations?

If you'd prefer her legal opinion, I'm with you.

Or take this situation: Let's say you visit your doctor with a medical condition. You describe all the symptoms. They run tests, do X-rays, and complete blood work. Finally, they call you to come into the office to discuss the findings. Do you prefer that your doctor simply provide you with all the tests and lab results, give a diagnosis, and identify possible treatments with the pros and cons of each? Or would you like the doctor's point of view about which treatment he recommends in your situation? Although you may decide to consider your options for a few days before making a final decision, I'm guessing you want an opinion—not just information.

And frankly, I know few doctors who would walk out of the consultation room, leaving you with only the raw information. That's what they get paid to do—give expert opinions.

People with presence have confidence in their recommendations and opinions. The top brass frequently interrupt hesitant briefers with a probe, "So what's your opinion on this?" If you're the expert, spit it out. Don't force others to ask your point or your conclusion.

Magazine editors agree that their most widely read section is typically the Letters to the Editor section. Opinions. Ask newspaper editors about their most widely read page. Again, they'll tell you it's the editorials: Opinions. Why are talk shows popular? Guests spout strong opinions. Agree or disagree—it doesn't matter. In fact, the more controversial, the better. Opinions get action and reaction.

Take a stand. Recommend. Drive a stake in the ground.

14

Think Like Hollywood

*Storytelling is the most powerful way to put ideas
into the world today. . . . Stories are the creative conversion of
life itself into a more powerful, clearer, more meaningful experience.
They are the currency of human contact.*

—ROBERT MCKEE

When my agent got a nibble from CBS to turn my first novel
into a movie, I immediately started researching tips on writing screenplays. To my surprise, I discovered that the typical two-
hour movie was captured in an average 100- to 110-page script.
How could that be? There I was slaving over business books that
required manuscripts of 250–300 pages when a two-hour movie
required only 110 pages! I called Mitch, my literary agent at the
time, to verify appropriate script length.

"Only 110 pages for a two-hour movie? How can that be? Is
that the rule of thumb?"

"True," he said. "And sometimes shorter. Depends on the
genre. Comedy or adventure movies run about 85 to 100 pages
because there's less dialogue."

"But that still doesn't seem plausible," I persisted. "Most dra-
mas are based on long novels—some on very long novels."

"Yes. But what it takes a novelist pages and pages to tell, a
movie can show in a second—with just a background setting or
someone's shrug or eye roll."

He made his point: Visuals replace myriad words.

Remember that when it comes to making your point with any audience of one or one thousand. Think visually.

Tell a Good Story

Steve Jobs organized one of his most famous speeches, often referred to as the "Stay hungry; stay foolish" speech, around three brief stories:[22]

> Thank you. I'm honored to be with you today for your commencement from one of the finest universities in the world. Truth be told, I never graduated from college and this is the closest I've ever gotten to a college graduation. Today I want to tell you three stories from my life. That's it. No big deal. Just three stories.
>
> The first story is about connecting the dots. . . .
> *[He tells a second story, then a third and ends with this:]*
>
> When I was young, there was an amazing publication called The Whole Earth Catalogue, which was one of the bibles of my generation. It was created by a fellow named Stuart Brand not far from here in Menlo Park, and he brought it to life with his poetic touch. This was in the late Sixties, before personal computers and desktop publishing, so it was all made with typewriters, scissors, and Polaroid cameras. It was sort of like Google in paperback form thirty-five years before Google came along. It was idealistic, overflowing with neat tools and great notions...
> On the back cover of their final issue was a photograph of an early morning country road, the kind you might find yourself hitchhiking on if you were so adventurous. Beneath were the words, "Stay hungry, stay foolish." It was their farewell message as they signed off. "Stay hungry, stay foolish." And I have always wished that for myself, and now, as you graduate to begin anew, I wish that for you. Stay hungry, stay foolish. Thank you all, very much.

Why pack your point in a good story? People can argue with facts all day. But they can't argue with your experience or your story. When you present your case as information, statistics, data to be digested, people move into analysis mode. Lights go on; wheels whir in an attempt to "take the other tack and prove you wrong." But when you offer an illustration or personal experience, they relax and listen for the idea.

Like a scriptwriter, think in themes, scenes, and storylines. Instead of laying out platitudes or lecturing about this or that, create a compelling story to get your point across. Stories include humorous anecdotes, slices of everyday life, success stories, or failure stories (use these to build trust and balance the picture about what you and your organization can and cannot do).

One thing to keep in mind in such stories: You should not always be the hero in your own stories. Let someone else "save the day" and shine with the heroic action that solves the customer's problem or gives the wise advice that pulls the misguided manager back from the brink of disaster.

> Why pack your point in a good story? People can argue with facts all day. But they can't argue with your experience or your story.

Run through your memory database and keep a log of your best stories and situations so you can retrieve them at a moment's notice to illustrate points in your area of expertise. You'll be amazed how often you find a chance to tell them while conversing with colleagues at the monthly birthday get-together, while greeting customers at a trade show, or during a meeting with VIPs at a networking dinner.

Think theme. Shakespeare had his twenty-six plot lines. Business storytellers have their favorite key themes and initiatives from year to year and decade to decade: "The Customer Is Always Right." "Content Is King." "Quality Is Our Number One Goal." "Nothing Happens Until Somebody Sells Something!" "David Versus Goliath." "People Are Our Most Valuable Asset." "Take Care of Your People and Your People Will Take Care of the Customer." "Innovate!" "Imagine Tomorrow." "Building Tomorrow's Leaders Today." "Never Give Up." "Change Never Ends."

With the theme in mind, identify an appropriate story to illustrate that point. What customer incident can you relate to your executive team to persuade them to act on your recommendations? What happened at the industry meeting that underscores to your colleagues the need for competitive intelligence sharing among them? What personal experience can you tell that helps your staff know what you value most in their performance? What tidbit of conversation did you overhear last week in the cafeteria that illustrates the team spirit in your division?

Once you have the story or incident in mind, practice telling it in a compelling way.

— *Identify the punch line.* That's where you end the story. Everything needs to build up to that point. Say the punch word in that punch line last.
— *Set up the story in an intriguing way.* Don't wave a flag by saying, "Let me tell you a story that illustrates why I think blah, blah, blah." Instead, try something like, "Honesty can kill your business. Last week I made the mistake of being honest with one of our suppliers about X. Then this Tuesday, I get a call from J.T. Wilbot, who says to me. . . ." And you're off into the story. Whatever setup you use should make people say, "Tell me more."
— *Keep the details relevant.* Just like the movie scriptwriter, use enough details so that your listener can picture what's happening. But omit details that contribute nothing to the setting, mood, or point.
— *Let us see the action.* To make the fullest impact, set your characters in motion. Let us hear them talk and see them act. As the storyteller, don't get between the audience and the action, merely telling us what *you* heard and saw earlier. Let people see for themselves—just as they do when sitting in the theatre. Re-create the scene and dialogue for them as you tell the story.

— *Transition to your point.*
So what's your point? Never tell us what the story means. Interpreting the punch line kills a good joke, and it'll also ruin a great story. Tell the story and stop. Be silent. Let the audience soak up its meaning. Then, and only then, bridge to your point in the presentation, conversation, or meeting.

> Storytellers hold the stage—and mindshare—longer than most people. Their stories typically deliver an emotional wallop that makes the point memorable and persuasive.

So how does storytelling add to your personal presence? Storytellers hold the stage—and mindshare—longer than most people. Their stories typically deliver an emotional wallop that makes the point memorable and persuasive.

Create the Movie Trailer with a Good Sound Bite

Movie trailers serve three purposes: They tempt audiences to see the movie. They capture the soul and spirit of the movie. Finally, they remind moviegoers what they've seen and felt long after they leave the theatre. Every time people see the movie advertised, hear about the forthcoming DVD release, learn about the novel upon which the book is based, or hear a friend tell how the novel differs from the screenplay, that trailer reminds them once again of what they saw on the screen. In a phrase or sentence, the trailer captures the meaning of the movie.

Sound bites serve a similar role. The more famous ones have lived on through the years, carrying with them the message and the context of the dream and the day:

Abraham Lincoln, at the memorial service for those who died in battle at Gettysburg, Pennsylvania, during the Civil War, November 19, 1863: "We here highly resolve that these dead shall not have died in vain—that this nation, under God, shall have a new birth of freedom—and that government of the people, by the people, for the people, shall not perish from the earth."

Patrick Henry to Virginia delegates in 1775: "Give me liberty or give me death."

Ronald Reagan to the people of West Berlin at the Brandenburg Gate (many considered this the beginning of the end of the Cold War): "Mr. Gorbachev, tear down this wall."

Martin Luther King, Jr. speaking in Washington D.C. on August 28, 1963: "I have a dream that one day this nation will rise up and live out the true meaning of its creed. . . ."

Steve Jobs to Pepsi's John Sculley in his persuasive appeal for him to join Apple in 1983 as its CEO: "Do you want to spend the rest of your life selling sugar water or do you want a chance to change the world?"

Avis's classic ad campaign: "We're number 2. We try harder."

Donald Trump's classic line in his long-playing TV series *The Apprentice*: "You're fired."

Hillary Clinton in her campaign for the White House: "I don't intend to play the gender card; I intend to play the winning card."

Bill O'Reilly on his nightly cable TV news show: "The spin stops here. We're looking out for you."

So how do you create a solid sound bite that everyone will remember after they sleep?

Get personal. Shape your message to fit your audience. What's their perspective on what you have to say? What do they want to know? What's their interest in the topic? What questions do they want answered by you? What solution do they want delivered? What promise do they want to hear? If it's on their mind, it needs to roll off your tongue: Answer the question. Solve the problem. Give the reason. Offer the explanation. Provide the backstory. Teach them something. Just make it about them.

Edit out the nonessential. Someone once asked Ernest Hemingway, "How do you write the Great American Novel?" He responded, "That's easy. Just sit down and type out your story. When you're finished, go back and cross out all the adjectives and adverbs." An oversimplification to be sure, but an excellent editing principle for sound bites. Cut articles (*a, an, the, that*) and limp language. Discard a weak verb propped up by an adverb or an adjective for a stronger verb. For example: "This will be an exciting new idea for your team" pops as "This new idea will excite your team."

Shape what remains. Use contrasts, triads, rhyming, alliteration, or puns to make your sound bite memorable. Play off frameworks already established through jokes, ads, or commercials. For example, Apple's "There's an app for that," or Coke's "It's the real thing," or Wendy's "Where's the beef?" or *Jerry Maguire's* "Show me the money!" Countless people have borrowed those frames to launch and anchor their own messages.

Let's say you're trying to motivate your sales team to increase efforts in building key relationships that could turn into strategic partnerships later. You might play with this frame: "We're paying for your trip to this global networking event, but in return I'm going to be expecting you to 'Show me the money'! Here's how . . ."

Another example using the Coca-Cola frame: In introducing someone to an audience, you may want to impress upon them his genuineness. You might say, "With Steve, there are no hidden agendas. He's the real thing."

Using the Apple frame and talking about the disorganization in your garage, you might say, "I'm planning a bonding experience with my teenager this weekend when we clean out the garage.

But he's probably going to tell me 'there's an app for that, Dad.'"
You get the idea. Such frames make everyday anecdotes and comments engaging.

Make Metaphors and Analogies Memorable

Movie critics love to look for hidden meanings in the movies they review.

The movie debuts. Movie critics try to tell us what we'll see and hear by drawing comparisons with what moviegoers know from the past. "It's like *The Perfect Storm* set in the context of marriage. All possible threats to a relationship collide at once on this once-happy couple and turn their life into a bitter struggle for survival."

Using metaphors and analogies, critics have a field day telling us what to expect on the screen. Based on how enticing their reviews turn out to be, audiences either flock to the movie or ignore it. (Obviously, some reviewers in the habit of delving for the movie writer's deep hidden meaning have never heard the American film producer Sam Goldwyn's philosophy: "If you want to send a message, use Western Union." The comment, of course, was to encourage writers to plot a great story and forget moralizing in their movies.)

But that is fiction and moviemaking. You're delivering business messages. Even so, analogies and metaphors will serve you well. They capture a concept in a few words and help people grasp and retain a complex idea by relating it to something they already understand.

"That project manual was so detailed that it was like a paint-by-numbers sketch book."

"Having a corporate account on Facebook feels like being on Ma Bell's party line."

Financial gurus Karen Berman and Joe Knight, in their excellent book *Financial Intelligence for Entrepreneurs*, use this analogy to explain operating expenses: "You can think of operating expenses as the cholesterol in a business. Good cholesterol makes you healthy, while bad cholesterol clogs your arteries. Good operating expenses make your business strong, and bad operating expenses drag down your bottom line and prevent you from taking advantage of business opportunities."[23]

A client of mine, a COO from a Canadian manufacturing company, developed an entire speech around an expansive analogy to reintroduce her organization to the industry through a series of conferences where she planned to speak to gain visibility. Because she had a background in the theatre during college and spent her spare time on the board of a local community theatre, she drew parallels between acting and preparing a company for an audit. Casting characters aligned with assigning roles/players to interact with the visiting auditors. Preparing the script aligned with updating policy manuals. And so forth. She drew nine key parallels between the theatre and auditing to make a memorable keynote address.

Metaphors and analogies never *prove* anything. But they do make your message memorable, persuasive, and unique.

Be the one who utters the sound bite, creates the metaphor, or establishes the analogy that positions your organization's message for years or decades to come. That's presence, and that's staying power!

15

. . . .

Learn to Think on Your Feet Under Pressure

. . . .

I've noticed two things about men who get big salaries.
They are almost invariably men who, in conversation
or in conference, are adaptable. They quickly get the
other fellow's view. They are more eager to do this than
to express their own ideas. Also, they state their own
point of view convincingly.
—JOHN HALLOCK

First, you hear yourself talking. Then all of a sudden you have an out-of-body experience, in which you're floating above yourself, hearing yourself babble on but unable to help yourself. Then this third voice shows up somewhere above your head, hearing both the first you babbling and the second you analyzing. The third voice says, "Self, snap it back together. You two are going to miss a beat. You can't keep up two tracks for long."

This dialogue in your head represents true pressure. If you can keep your poise and avoid revealing the split personality to anyone during such an episode, you're ready to tackle most situations with confidence. But no matter how prepared you are, if the dialogue goes on long enough and the pressure becomes strong enough, your brain can freeze. It's at those times that you need techniques to think clearly under pressure.

The greatest pressure typically comes when you're asked a question. Nothing strikes fear in the heart of those less prepared than to hear, "If you don't mind, we'd like to ask you a few questions." Sometimes, you can plan for the pressure because you're giving a formal presentation and have been told to allow time for Q&A at the end.

On other occasions, the pressure comes at a time of crisis—personal tragedy that overwhelms your emotional circuits or an organizational crisis when the media swarms around you, abuzz with microphones and cameras. Your recorded or printed words will set the course of action for many people for a long time. And you'll have a short prep time.

Respondents to our Booher survey considered the ability to think on their feet the skill they most needed to improve to increase their credibility. Here's my best advice to tackle that challenge.

Don't Dribble While You Decide

Coach Wimbish made us dribble Figure 8s until we were ready to drop in our tracks because she wanted us to master control of the ball as we threaded our way toward the basketball goal for a layup shot. But in a game, our dribbling often got us in trouble. Because we were good at it, we dribbled too much and missed opportunities to pass the ball to a teammate open for a shot. In my mind's eye, I can still see and hear Coach Wimbish shouting from the sidelines: "Get your head up. Look around. *Pass* the ball!"

"But nobody was open," someone would protest to her when we'd huddle at the sidelines. "Then just hold the ball until they *get* open," she'd say. "Dribbling is a last resort. Get open, or pass the ball!"

We'd return to the court. Sure enough, somebody would forget her admonition, start to dribble, and the opponent would steal the ball. Once again, Coach Wimbish would lunge off the bench and shout, "Get your head up. Look around. *Pass* the ball!" Of course, you can't play basketball without dribbling. But we understood her point: Far too often, dribbling became a habit, and we failed to take advantage of the fast breaks and opportunities.

The same happens in business situations. We're asked for a project update or an opinion and we dribble rather than think how best to use the opportunity to make a point. Out of habit, we open our mouth and drivel while we decide what we really want to say.

Instead, as Coach Wimbish advised, practice the pause. While you collect your thoughts, remain silent. Forgo the word fillers (*uh, umm, well, you know, ah*). Simply pause. Look reflective. Restate the stem of the question or begin with a common truth. Then after you decide what point you want to make, give your update or your opinion.

> Muggers attack people meandering aimlessly, seemingly unaware of their surroundings. Talkers who ramble aimlessly invite attackers for the same reason: They're easy targets for interruptions, disagreements, and distractions that get them off track. The pause is powerful. Use it to increase attention and credibility for your "reasoned" comments.

The danger of not thinking before you speak can be far more serious in work situations than in basketball.

The police tell us that criminals look for easy targets. To avoid being their victim, the police advise walking with purpose. Before leaving a building at night, know where you parked, have your keys in your hands, and walk briskly to your car. Muggers attack people meandering aimlessly, seemingly unaware of their surroundings. Talkers who ramble aimlessly invite attackers for the same reason: They're easy targets for interruptions, disagreements, and distractions that get them off track.

The pause is powerful. Use it to increase attention and credibility for your "reasoned" comments.

Respond Rather Than React to Questions

In the 2008 presidential campaign, Sarah Palin took some of her harshest criticism for her interview with Katie Couric. In that interview, one particular habit stands out most frequently in Palin's responses: She reacted to the tone and responded far too quickly. For example:

> *Couric:* When it comes to establishing your worldview, I was curious. What newspapers and magazines did you regularly read before you were tapped for this—to stay informed and to understand the world?
>
> *Palin:* I've read most of them, again with a great appreciation for the press, for the media.
>
> *Couric:* What, specifically?
>
> *Palin:* Um, all of them, any of them that have been in front of me all these years.
>
> *Couric:* Can you name a few?
>
> *Palin:* I have a vast variety of sources where we get our news, too. Alaska isn't a foreign country, where it's kind of suggested, "Wow, how could you keep in touch with what the rest of Washington, D. C., may be thinking when you live up there in Alaska?" Believe me, Alaska is like a microcosm of America.

In later interviews when Palin was asked to critique her own performance in that interview, she said, "I felt insulted with the question. I took her question to mean '*Do* you read?'"

Had Palin taken her time to gather her thoughts before responding, she could have easily responded to that question in Couric's interview. If she had wanted to answer vaguely, she might have responded, "I read publications that give me a broad view of the world—some are conservative in their views and some are more liberal." That broad statement would have given her more thinking time if Couric had pressed with a follow-up for specifics. Or, she could have bridged to make a different point: "I read publications that give me a broad view of the world—some are conservative in their views and some are liberal. But actually, I find that interacting with people face-to-face and online gives me a much more informed view of what the average person is thinking and feeling."

Had she wanted to be both specific and gracious (what I recommend) during a hostile interview, she might have responded, "I read several things to stay up to date. Those that I find particularly helpful are . . ."

Never react to the tone of questions—whether accusatory, hostile, or sarcastic questions from a boss, client, colleague, or the media. Ignore the "hot words," and treat them as objective questions. Strong emotions and pressure to respond quickly can freeze your brain. Pause, look reflective as you gather your thoughts, and then respond to the question or bridge to the point you want to make.

Unload the Loaded Questions

Surgeons at a large research hospital with which I consult frequently receive loaded questions from reporters, who often have an agenda. The reporter may want to make the case that the hospital should be doing more organ transplants when those organs are available from countries such as China, where citizens sell their body organs for cash. A reporter asked this loaded question of a physician: "Didn't your colleague, in effect, doom Baby X to death by not accepting the proffered organ that was available from China, even at a price that his parents were willing to pay?"

Notice that the premise of the question is that the choice about the morality of buying and selling organs was the physician's. Answering such a loaded question puts you in a losing situation. To respond, simply state your position on the issue without directly referring to the way the question was asked: "We believe organ donation should be a voluntary practice for several reasons. [Name them]. . . ."

Or, you can more pointedly say, "I don't agree with your premise. My position on that issue is X." Never make the mistake of repeating a faulty premise.

Anticipate and Prepare for Questions

Almost without exception, when I'm advising a sales group on responding to questions during a sales call, they can quickly list the typical questions customers ask about their product or service. After they list those ten to fifteen questions, I pose this question to the sales team: Somebody give me your typical response to Question A. There's a rumble around the room for a few seconds. Then finally somebody says, "Well, I don't know that we have a single answer. I guess it varies from time to time."

"Okay, let's try to answer the second question you just listed. If this question comes up all the time from your customers, how do you answer it?" Again, a mumble-jumble. Someone takes a stab at it. Then a colleague "corrects" him. Then another colleague "adds" to the response. Then maybe another speaks up to revise what the previous colleague said with, "No, you don't ever want to say that because some customers will be offended that blah-blah-blah. We've found we get a better customer response when we explain it like this . . ."

You get the picture: A sales team has spent hundreds of hours learning to position their product against the competition but obviously no time in anticipating and perfecting answers for routine questions that come up every time they talk to customers.

This situation could be labeled sales malpractice: sizzle without the question substance. If you're in sales, put yourself in scenarios where colleagues fire product or service questions at you until you can think on your feet well enough to answer those questions with substance.

To be clear, brief, and consistent, be prepared.

Use The SEER Format® as a Guide

I recommend The SEER Format® for thinking on your feet (contact Booher Consultants, www.booher.com, for more information about training programs) in almost any impromptu situation that calls for an opinion or response—particularly to your executive leadership team or a client:

S: Summary   Summarize your answer, opinion, or update in a sentence.

E: Elaboration   Elaborate with the reasons, data, criteria, explanations, or whatever supports your summary.

E: Example   Provide an illustration or anecdote to connect emotionally and make your response memorable. The more concrete and specific, the better.

R: Restatement   Restate your answer in a sentence.

Here's an example to illustrate the structure:

Question: "If we were to hire you for this position, what do you think would be your *primary* contribution?"

Summary: From what you've told me, I think my primary contribution here will be project management.

Elaboration: Although several experiences from past positions align with what you've described, your biggest headache now seems to be budget overruns, delays with suppliers, late deliveries to your clients, and staff squabbles. For the past seven years, that's what I've spent my time doing—supervising a group of twelve systems analysts at Prescott with projects that lasted sometimes six to twelve months, managing an inhouse warehouse system in Cincinnati that supplied the entire country (including inventory and ordering), and then managing the consulting projects with Brasco—projects ranging from $5–10 million in revenue.

Example: For example, at Brasco, I remember a project where we handled a client move from New York to Plano, Texas, for 7,800 people—securing the office space, ordering the furniture from four different manufacturers, and handling the actual move. We got it done two days early—and $18,000 under budget. In fact, that client has used us twice since then for relocations of other offices.

Restatement: So definitely, my project management skills in bringing projects in on time and within budget will be something I think you'll find of immediate value here.

The structure builds your credibility because the four segments meet all three of Aristotle's criteria for persuasion: logos (logic), ethos (trustworthiness), and pathos (empathy). The elaboration meets the listener's need for logic as you speak. The example provides the emotional connection with your listeners. And the straightforward one-sentence summary and restatement underscore your integrity or trustworthiness by conveying your intention to be clear.

Consider this format for a fifteen-second response during Q&A or a fifteen-minute update when the boss unexpectedly calls on you during a meeting to provide a project status. The more you practice this format, the less pressure you'll feel when thinking on your feet and speaking in impromptu situations.

Understand the Power of Well-Phrased Questions

Those with less sense of self think that they must always be in control. Consequently, you'll often hear them in lecture mode with phrases such as "Let me be clear." "The fact of the matter is . . ." "You can be sure that . . ." "Here's what I want you to do." These phrases can make you sound like a bully in a manager role.

Questions, on the other hand, invite others into a conversation while you provide coaching and guidance rather than criticism. Examples: "How did you think that project turned out?" "What would you like to do differently next time?" "Do you have ideas about how to cut expenses on future trips?" "What are your plans to achieve that goal?" "In light of these numbers and the company initiatives for the quarter, what do you think should be the highest priority for this month?"

. . . .

Inviting questions, moderating your tone, and phrasing evenly position you as a coach and critical thinker rather than judge and jury. Judges and juries generate fear while coaches earn admiration and respect.

. . . .

High visibility. Low tolerance for mistakes. The chance that your words will have a long shelf life. The next time that's the case and you have an out-of-body experience, expect the voice floating above your head to say, "Nice job."

Inviting questions, moderating your tone, and phrasing evenly position you as a coach and critical thinker rather than judge and jury. Judges and juries generate fear while coaches earn admiration and respect.

Once again, presence comes from others' perspective of your leadership.

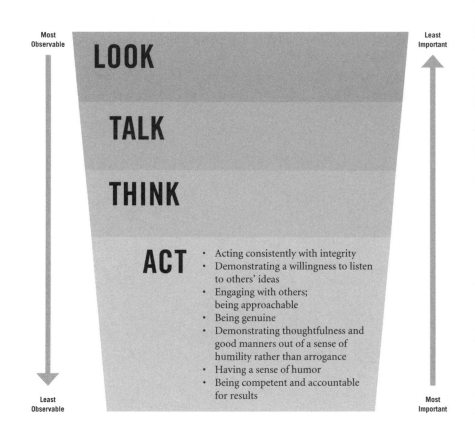

Most Observable

Least Important

LOOK

TALK

THINK

ACT

- Acting consistently with integrity
- Demonstrating a willingness to listen to others' ideas
- Engaging with others; being approachable
- Being genuine
- Demonstrating thoughtfulness and good manners out of a sense of humility rather than arrogance
- Having a sense of humor
- Being competent and accountable for results

Least Observable

Most Important

PART 4: HOW YOU ACT

16

....

Engage Emotionally

....

They may forget what you said,
but they will never forget how you made them feel.
—CAROL BUECHNER

"We can't hear you," one of the workers yelled out from the rubble when President George W. Bush started to speak impromptu from the top of a fire truck as he toured the damage from the 9-11 attack at the World Trade Center.

"Well I can hear you. The whole world hears you. And the people who knocked down these buildings will hear from all of us soon."

His comment connected with the hearts of Americans who were feeling the same raw emotions. Many say that was the day he became their president; it marked the height of his popularity. Opponents continued to label him personally likeable even if growing weary of the war and his policies toward the end of his two terms in office.

John Kerry, on the other hand, was much criticized for his artificial greeting at the Democratic National Convention when he stepped to the lectern, saluted, and said, "I'm John Kerry, and I'm reporting for duty." Rehearsed. Unemotional. Disconnected.

President Barack Obama experienced the same learning curve

about emotional engagement. At his 2008 inauguration, the emotional connection was high as the country watched its first African American president and wife Michelle stroll down Pennsylvania Avenue greeting well-wishers. But after those early months when he self-admittedly struggled to stay in touch with the American people, his popularity ratings declined. Americans want their leaders to engage with them, not just poll them. Employees want their executives to listen to them, not just assign projects or sign paychecks. Clients want their suppliers to care about their business challenges, not just sell products or services to them.

Those who have presence strive to engage emotionally as well as physically.

But emotional presence implies permission.

Few people will permit you to barge in on them at will. In fact, life in the fast lane requires us to set our default drive to tune people out literally and figuratively. So what is it that makes people invite you into their life, so to speak?

Two things: credibility and likeability. You may be credible and have others pick your brain and benefit from your work—but choose not to be around you if they don't have to be. On the other hand, you may be a likeable, life-of-the-party sort whom everybody wants to hang out with. But people may not consider you credible in challenging times for critical information or competent performance.

The combination of both competence and likeability characterizes a leader with presence. That's why political pollsters construct survey questions to attempt to measure the candidates' likeability ratings as well as their competence scores.

The perception of both leads to presence and the presidency.

Likeability may be hard to define, but we know it when we feel it. We like those who show interest in us and are interesting themselves. We like those who are familiar to us, similar to us, trustworthy, genuine, transparent, humble, positive, and accepting of us.[24]

So how do you demonstrate likeability?

Approach Others: Aim to Give Attention Rather Than Get Attention

The tagline "mover and shaker" comes from a metaphor—a very visual component of a personality trait or habit. Not only do these people move through many networks, work a lot of relationships, and shake their share of hands, they literally take the lead in approaching people. When newcomers enter a room, people with presence approach them confidently, introduce themselves, act as host, make introductions, and connect them to others in the group. They approach and give attention to others.

Unlike wallflowers who remain self-conscious and stand to the side, looking as though they're about to wilt, people with presence put themselves on the frontline to serve. As a result, others feel their presence because of the attention they give—not receive.

Consider what you see when looking in a handheld mirror. Hold the mirror at arm's length, and your image is small. Bring the mirror closer and closer to your face, and your image grows until it seems to engulf you. To have this same "larger than life" effect on others, take the lead in approaching them—to introduce yourself, to shake hands, to wish them well, and to say goodbye as they leave a meeting.

Be Approachable

A title in the *HBR List* recently intrigued me: "Just Because I'm Nice, Don't Assume I'm Dumb."[25] Harvard Business professor and author Amy J.C. Cuddy points out that many managers make the snap judgment that likeability and competence are mutually exclusive. That may explain why some people remain aloof from those they serve and with whom they work.

Exclusivity is not a new idea. More than five hundred years ago, Machiavelli had the same idea when he studied the link between fear and power. People do pay attention to those with power to reward or punish them. But people *enjoy* being around those who are likeable, humble, and willing to give them the proverbial time of day.

. . . .

People do pay attention to those with power to reward or punish them. But people *enjoy* being around those who are likeable, humble, and willing to give them the proverbial time of day.

. . . .

At my nephew's recent wedding reception, the best man delivered a humorous, yet poignant, toast to the bride and groom. To watch him interact with the other guests later in the evening, it would have been difficult to guess he was an oncologist at a prestigious cancer center. No pretension. Genuine interest in others.

A celebrity ESPN sports commentator hosts the weekend games on TV, and then sits quietly in the audience at his church when he's in town applauding appreciatively when various amateurs speak from the stage. No pretension around others of less renown.

These people remain approachable, and friends admire them for their character—not just their notoriety.

Listen Like You Mean It

You can demonstrate that you're listening in four key ways: (1) Using attentive body language; (2) Asking questions; (3) Answering questions; (4) Taking action on what you've heard.

To build rapport as you listen, make mirroring a conscious choice. Yawning is one form of unconscious mirroring familiar to most of us. See someone yawn, and before you know it, you're yawning. You walk into a room where everybody's whispering, and automatically you lower your voice to a whisper to sync with those around you. Someone passing you in the hallway nods and smiles; you automatically return the nod and smile. These are examples of subconscious mirroring.

To make others feel accepted and to create a bond, consciously mirror their body language and match their speaking rate and pattern. Mirroring facial expressions with men, however, doesn't work so well because they often have an expressionless face. So if you're a woman who has ever been told you are "too expressive" or "too transparent" with your face, then when listening to men, keep a serious face to be considered more intelligent and seasoned. Men listening to a woman should mirror her expression to demonstrate listening. Give the speaker your full attention. Stop whatever you're doing and look the speaker directly in the eye. Tilt your head slightly to one side. The literal message is, "I'm giving you an ear."

Ask questions about what the speaker is saying to help clarify thoughts and to verify that you've heard correctly and have drawn the intended conclusions. Answer questions specifically rather than vaguely. Follow through with action to demonstrate that you've heard and agree with what someone has asked you to do.

After all, how frustrated do you become when you have to call a credit-card company, insurance agency, or healthcare facility several times to take care of an invoice that should have been corrected with your initial call if the representative had only listened to you the first time? Such interactions happen only once or twice with the same individual. But imagine the negative impression created when poor listening becomes habitual with colleagues over an extended period of time.

Benjamin Disraeli was right when he observed, "Talk to a man about himself and he will listen for hours." The magic in this mix? He or she will think you are a remarkable person. Listening increases likeability, and likeability leads to trust.

Express Empathy

Noted psychologist William Ickes, at the University of Texas, has studied empathy in depth and writes this: "Empathetically accurate perceivers are those who are consistently good at 'reading' other people's thoughts and feelings. All else being equal, they are likely to be the most tactful advisors, the most diplomatic officials, the most effective negotiators, the most electable politicians, the most productive salespersons, the most successful teachers, and the most insightful therapists."[26]

I had occasion to hear a staffer at the Department of Defense Finance and Accounting Service talk with pride about one of the agency's key achievements: the ability to get fast cash to military families in need during recent flooding incidents on the Louisiana coast. Her body language and voice suggested deep empathy with families she'd served personally while issuing checks on-site along the coast.

To empathize with others, you have to know and understand their situation. Find commonalities. Instead of asking people the age-old question, "So what do you do?" probe with, "So tell me about your work" or "Tell me what you're involved in currently." When they respond in some global or vague way, ask: "For example?" Deal in specifics. Dig for the details. Demonstrate your interest.

Comment on the commonplace. Ask an opinion about the event. Ask about others' comfort or discomfort with the setting, about the food served, about the entertainment, about how they know other guests. Ask about their plans for the upcoming week, or weekend, or vacation, or next project, or current challenge. Listen to their responses, and make your comments and questions genuine.

Consider the Toothbrush Test

No matter how much people like you, they probably don't want to share their toothbrush with you. Take care not to violate others' sense of personal space.

Familiarity leads to liking. But familiarity may also lead to a diminished sense of respect. Remember the facetious definition of a consultant? Someone who carries a bigger briefcase and travels more than a hundred miles from home. Think of it this way: You let your teen call you on your cell at 2:00 a.m., but you may not give that same freedom to your Facebook friends or your florist.

Consider the physical side of the toothbrush test. More formally, Dr. Edward Hall calls this principle of personal space the study of proxemics. The *intimate* zone is 6–18 inches. Only those very close to us emotionally can enter here—lovers, family, pets. The *personal* zone, between 18–48 inches, is the distance we stand from someone at an office party or PTA meeting. The *social* zone,

> Familiarity leads to liking. But familiarity may also lead to a diminished sense of respect.

between 4 and 12 feet, represents the distance we typically allow between us and strangers or those we don't know very well such as a repair person or the store clerk. The *public* zone, more than 12 feet, is where we stand to speak to a group. Women tend to stand somewhat closer and men tend to stand somewhat farther apart. Distance also varies in different cultures.

Violate these unwritten rules by invading somebody's space and they will consider you aggressive and intimidating. You have used their toothbrush. They may not tell you directly to get your iPad off their desk or to stop waving your arm in their face, but they will shut down emotionally. If both of you are standing, the other person will step back. If you follow, they will take another step away. The dance begins.

> Take it easy with touching and realize the message of dominance you may be sending. These may trigger emotional detachment rather than engagement.

While touch may communicate caring with close friends, touch also conveys status in our society. It's a sign of dominance— a handshake, a touch to the arm or shoulder, a brush against someone passing in the hallway. Take it easy with touching and realize the message of dominance you may be sending. These may trigger emotional detachment rather than engagement.

Associate Yourself with the Popular and Pleasant

Besides the physical aspects of space and touching, consider emotional space. That is, to maintain your presence, associate yourself emotionally with the pleasant—and distance yourself from the unpleasant and unpopular.

This principle of emotional association comes into play every day in the marketing world. Advertisers use beautiful models to sell their cars, sports celebrities to endorse training equipment, and doctors to sell medical equipment or pharmaceuticals. Nonprofits invite celebrities to lend their name to their cause as honorary chairs for their fundraising charity events.

Robert Cialdini, in his excellent book *Influence*, writes at length about his research regarding the principle of association. He points out research in the areas of everyday life that you've probably experienced for yourself. For example, the principle of association is at play when radio stations announce their call letters immediately before they play the biggest hit songs of the day. When fans talk about their local college or pro sport team, it's "we won" during a winning season, but "they lost" during a losing season. Weather forecasters get blamed for the bad weather they predict.[27]

The cliché "Don't shoot the messenger" warns about human nature and this principle of association. Whether glory or blame, the reflection falls on those nearby. So pay attention to whom and with what you associate yourself.

Become an expert. And as Virgil says, "Follow an expert" until you do. Be present and engage others when and where good things happen.

17

Master Modesty and Mind Your Manners

Of the billionaires I have known, money just brings out the basic traits in them. If they were jerks before they had money, they are simply jerks with a billion dollars.

—WARREN BUFFETT

Armed with an undergraduate degree in engineering from Texas A&M, Dave seemed to be on the brink of disaster. He had applied to graduate school at several A-list universities and had been turned down by all of them. Grades gave him no problem at all. Attitude proved to be the barrier when he showed up for his interview with the admissions committee or dean. Finally, he got a call from Dartmouth. Considering it might be his last opportunity, Dave's parents called in a colleague of mine as his coach to prepare for the entrance interview process.

"So why are you having such a hard time?" his coach asked him.

"I don't like people," Dave told her.

"Why?"

"They're stupid."

"All of them?"

"All of them." The rest of their get-acquainted session proved to be quite revealing. Dave had had difficulty all his life because of his antisocial behavior. A brilliant individual but a loner, he did and said whatever he thought and felt.

His psychologist coach gave him an assignment for the next day's call-in phone session with her. "By tomorrow I want you to think of one person you like and be ready to tell me one positive thing about them."

"I can't."

"I'm sure you can if you give it some thought. You'll have overnight."

He called in at the appointed time the next morning. "I thought of somebody," he said. "My brother."

"Great." His coach was pleased. "What do you have positive to say about him? What's his strength?"

"He's kin to me."

Dave was dead serious. It had taken him more than twenty-four hours to come up with that distinguishing strength. Fortunately for Dave, however, after several more sessions with his coach, he aced the interview and won admission to Dartmouth.

Dave was diagnosed in his early teens with Asperger's syndrome, a condition characterized by significant difficulties in social interaction. But my point in telling you his story is this: Though Dave's bluntness in the above conversation sounds bizarre and atypical, the arrogant behavior is not.

> Rudeness, which often stems from arrogance, runs rampant in our culture. But people with presence live lives of civility. They stand out in a crowd of rude people.

Rudeness, which often stems from arrogance, runs rampant in our culture. But people with presence live lives of civility. They stand out in a crowd of rude people.

Be Gadget Gracious

In this attention-deficit culture, rudeness gets excused as multi-tasking: carrying on a face-to-face conversation while checking your email on your iPhone or sending a text. Microsoft's "Really" TV ad campaign depicts people checking their email or text messages in all kinds of inappropriate places: while in the toilet, at dinner with a date, walking down a crowded stairway. Exasperated onlookers deliver the simple punch line: "Really?" Although the subtext implies the absurdity of it all, it's far too real to raise eyebrows.

If you work in such a culture, all you have to do to increase your presence is to be present. That is, when you talk to people, show up. Put down your Blackberry, Android, or iPhone and make eye contact. Listen to people when they talk to you. If you work in an email-only culture, call people to resolve an issue in two minutes that would otherwise take a five-email exchange over four days. Meet with them face to face. You may be surprised how much you'll increase your influence over someone when you're fully present and engaged.

> In this attention-deficient culture, rudeness gets excused as multitasking: If you work in such a culture, all you have to do to increase your presence is to be present. . . . You may be surprised how much you'll increase your influence over someone when you're fully present and engaged.

Remember what you used to think of people who shook your hand at a cocktail party while glancing over your shoulder to see if someone more important had come through the door? That's the feeling others get if you're glancing at your gadgets while they're trying to gain your attention about an upcoming gambit for a new project or proposal. Often all it takes in the midst of this mass rudeness is to decide to be deliberate when listening to colleagues.

Exit Networking Discussions with Confidence

At mix-and-mingle events, don't overstay your welcome with any one person. Chat with them five to fifteen minutes (depending on the length of the entire event), and then move on. As you wrap up your conversation, say goodbye simply and briefly. Start talking in the past tense: "It has been nice talking with you and hearing about X." "It was great to meet you. Now I know why Kim speaks so highly of the Finance division." "I'd love to talk further with you about this sometime. I may give you a call or at least look you up at the next meeting." "Do you have a card? I'd like to have your contact information on file." "It's been nice getting to know you. I'm going to look you up on LinkedIn and see what other groups and people we have in common."

Then shake hands and make your exit. There's no need to make an excuse that you need to refresh your beverage, catch another person before they walk out the door, or go to the buffet table unless that's the case. People expect conversations to end. That's the purpose. Talk and walk.

Follow Protocol in Mixing Business with Pleasure

Because of the heavy demands on their time, executives blend their social and work lives, often building their personal relationships through business contacts, and vice versa. As the old saying goes, people do business with people they like. Be the liaison who brings people together over breakfast, lunch, dinner, golf games, committee work, or causes. Deal discussions follow as a by-product.

Make sure you're comfortable in such social settings and understand the protocol and rules of etiquette in each of these situations: Introductions. Timing and appropriateness of business topics. Appropriate dress. Who arrives first. Who pays. It's the little things done right that shout "class."

Basic Rules of Business Etiquette

Q. When business colleagues dine, who pays?
A. *Whoever extends the invitation pays. Of course, it's always in good taste to offer to pay. (The exception to this basic rule is when peers dine together routinely and pay for their own meals.)*

Q. Should you take a hostess gift when invited to a business colleague's home for dinner or an event?

A. *Yes. Food, beverage, flowers, or a small home decor item (such as a candle or picture frame) are appropriate.*

Q. Who should arrive first when dining out? Is it fashionable to arrive late?

A. *The host should arrive first. Punctuality distinguishes a person of class. Making a grand entrance by arriving "fashionably" late may be great PR for movie stars, but it never marks good manners for the business scene. Lack of punctuality shows disregard for others' time.*

Q. When is it appropriate to talk business when you're meeting with a colleague for a meal?

A. *Customs vary here from culture to culture. In some cultures, business discussions never begin until the meal has concluded. Westerners typically get to business discussions much sooner—after the first course. If it's a casual lunch together and you're having only one course, the discussion may start even sooner—but never before rapport-building chitchat.*

Q. When should you exchange business cards?

A. *Customs vary from culture to culture. In some countries, business cards are presented upon first meeting. It's an insult not to take them, read them carefully, and treat them respectfully (never use them for note-taking). In Western cultures, business cards are exchanged upon leaving as a "by the way" act—or exchanged during the discussion and used for notes.*

Q. Should you exchange business cards during a meal?

A. *No. Exchange cards either before or after the meal.*

Q. When and how should you send thank-you notes?

A. *Thank-you notes always suggest good taste. Send them after a job interview, an appointment, a party, a hosted meal, or any time you want to be remembered as a person with good manners. Traditionally, a thank-you note was always handwritten and mailed. Today, they are often* *emailed. Most importantly, they should be prompt, sincere, and brief.*

Q. When introducing people, who introduces who to whom?
A. *The person whose name you call first is the person you're honoring. Introduce a younger person to a more senior person, a junior colleague to a senior colleague, a coworker to a client, and so forth. Example: "Mr. Boss, I'd like to introduce my son to you." "Ms. VIP Client, this is Tom. He's been working on your project behind the scenes."*

Q. Is it appropriate to wear perfume or cologne at work?
A. *Yes, but make sure it's subtle. Cheap fragrances are strong and offensive. Keep in mind that some people are allergic to fragrances.*

Q. Is it appropriate to apply lipstick at the table after a meal or in public places?
A. *No. Go to a private place.*

Q. Is it appropriate for men to wear hats or caps when entering homes, restaurants, theatres, or places of worship?
A. *No. Hats and caps are appropriate outside and at sporting events even inside large indoor facilities.*

Q. When should you shake hands?
A. *Shaking hands is the typical business greeting to show goodwill in the Western culture. If for some reason you are unsure about a relationship, you may want to wait to see if the other person extends a hand first.*

NOTE: For an extended discussion on how these rules and others may vary from culture to culture, see my book *Communicate with Confidence: How to Say It Right the First Time and Every Time.*

Earn Your Seat at the Table

Your professionalism and poise when dining extends the perception of your presence on many fronts—as a representative of your organization or a self-assured individual comfortable in any setting. Learn and keep in mind the rules of basic dining etiquette so friends and colleagues can "dress you up and take you out." Dine with confidence so you can digest with ease.

The Down-and-Dirty Rules of Dining Etiquette

1. Never play the shuffle. Remember BMW. That is, never sit down to the table and wonder aloud, "Is this your bread plate or mine?" "Sorry, did I pick up your water glass?" The proper placement of items before you from left to right will always be B(bread), M(meal), W(water). Select and use them accordingly.

2. Keep the table clear of clutter. Place keys, cell phones, handbags, hats, briefcases, and so forth under your chair, in an empty chair, or on the floor.

3. Pay attention to posture. Sit up straight and bring your food to your mouth rather than slumping over the table and lowering your mouth to your food.

4. Pace your eating to that of your companions so that you're not noticeably faster or slower.

5. Place your napkin (folded in half with the fold toward your body) in your lap during the meal. If you have to leave the table during the meal, place your napkin in your chair and push your chair under the table. When you finish your meal, place the napkin loosely to the left of your plate.

6. Select your flatware from the outside inward toward the plate as you proceed through the meal. If your salad is served at the same time as your entree, eat your salad with your dinner fork. Once you pick up a utensil, never return it to the table again, but instead keep it on the plate. When you finish with your meal, place your utensils across the plate at an angle, with the tips of the utensils at ten o'clock and the handles at four o'clock (as if the plate were a clock face).

7. Cut only one bite of food at a time.

8. Pass the salt and pepper shakers together. If someone asks you to "pass the salt," ask if they would like the pepper also.

9. Pass food (bread, dessert, family-style dishes) from left to right.

10. Never chew with your mouth open or talk with food in your mouth.

Put Others at Ease

Your stock rises as the anxiety of those around you declines. When a client or colleague breaches some rule of etiquette, never call attention to their mistake by trying to correct them. If they fail to introduce you properly, introduce yourself. If they eat your dinner roll by mistake, do without your bread for the meal. If they don't know how to exit a networking group, walk them over to introduce them to another group nearby.

No one likes to feel inadequate, ill-prepared, incapable, or uninformed. Whatever you can do to lessen someone's discomfort and help them feel accepted, smart, and capable will increase their perception of your own presence and wisdom.

> Your stock rises as the anxiety of those around you declines. . . .
> No one likes to feel inadequate, ill-prepared, incapable, or uninformed.

Drop Arrogant Phrases from Your Vocabulary

Arrogant language can become habit-forming. Rather than sounding authoritative, it sounds merely judgmental, offending those to whom it's directed. Look at the following examples and consider the difference in the ways the statements come across.

Which person would you rather carry on a conversation with during a three-hour flight? If you select the tactful speaker, I'm with you.

Arrogant Vs. Tactful Language

"Let me be perfectly clear . . ." *(patronizing, sounds like parent to child)* **vs.** "I want to emphasize . . ."

"I must inform you that . . ." *(overly formal and stuffy)* **vs.** "I want to let you know that . . ."

"I contend that . . ." *(emphasizes contention and conflict)* **vs.** "I believe that . . ." Or simply state the opinion without this introductory phrase.

"How can I phrase this so you don't misunderstand?" *(emphasizes the other person is the dummy)* **vs.** "I want to explain this clearly." Or simply restate your information or opinion in a clearer way.

"You're wrong." *(positions the other person in error)* **vs.** "I disagree." Or: "I have a different opinion on that." Or: "My information on that differs. . . ."

"Not true." *(positions an opinion as fact)* **vs.** "I don't see it that way."

"The facts prove otherwise." *(authoritarian tone that positions the other person in error)* **vs.** "The facts I have differ."

Rid Yourself of Arrogant Body Language

Arrogant body language can be just as off-putting as arrogant language. Such classic poses as a lifted chin convey an attitude of disdain you may not intend. (For a fuller discussion of the message your body language conveys, see Chapter 5.)

Another expression of arrogance is staking out a claim to territory by taking over public pathways—to the water cooler, to the snack bar, to the training room. Arrogant people stand in the doorway to the boardroom or the conference room, blocking others' entrance and forcing them to go around or ask permission to enter. They claim territory by tossing their jacket over extra chairs in the meeting room or by scattering their gadgets or papers around them on the meeting table. These displays say, "I'm staking my claim to this public property because my rights and needs are superior to all others'."

These acts of arrogance build resentment rather than respect.

Gracious behavior and simple courtesies nourish our spirit. Rudeness robs our time-is-money society of enjoyment and diminishes individual distinction. Good manners are a mark of modesty and class.

Golda Meir, the former Israeli prime minister, once quipped, "Don't be so humble; you're not that great." Follow that thinking in the reverse: Develop your personal presence and reputation to such greatness that you leave room for modesty and manners.

18

....

Lighten Up
Without Letting Down

....

A keen sense of humor helps us to overlook
the unbecoming, understand the unconventional,
tolerate the unpleasant, overcome the unexpected,
and outlast the unbearable.

—BILLY GRAHAM

Jonas comes tiptoeing into the bedroom at midnight after finishing his moonlighting job at The Ball Park at Arlington. Although he pulls a day job as an accountant, his second job contributes to the fun in his life—by including free admission to all the Texas Ranger games. His friend Bo, as a small business owner and equipment supplier to the team, hangs around with him to watch the game after the work's done.

Already asleep at midnight, Jonas's wife wakes up to ask him, "How was the game?"

"You wouldn't believe it if I told you. Just go back to sleep, and I'll explain it in the morning." She did and he did.

It seems that shortly after Hall-of-Fame pitcher and all-time MLB leader in no-hitters Nolan Ryan, current owner of the Texas Rangers, outbid Mark Cuban, Maverick owner, for the baseball team, he and his investors threw a big pregame bash at the stadium to celebrate. They invited all the MLB coaches and players to join them. Both former presidents, George H.W. Bush and son

George W., himself a former owner of the Texas Rangers, joined them for the event.

The PR people gathered the press for the photo op. Presidents, Secret Service agents, MLB coaches, and a multitude of the famous players in the league arrived in the reception room. The head honcho marketing guy tells Nolan Ryan and the two presidents to form a receiving line, which they did—right beside where Jonas and his friend Bo just happened to be standing. All of a sudden, the first athlete is shaking their hands. "Good to meet you." And the next. And the next: "Nice to see you." And the line of pro players and celebrity coaches keeps coming.

George, George, Nolan, Jonas, and Bo. Plus the two Secret Service agents behind them. About the seventh or eighth person who sticks out a hand to introduce himself, the outliers stop trying to explain that they don't belong in the receiving line and just enjoy themselves.

"Hi, I'm Bo. Nice to meet you, Brett."

"Good to meet you, Coach."

"Glad you could stop by, Josh."

"Tony, good to meet you."

Rather than getting uptight that someone would accuse them of crashing the party of star-studded guests when they accidentally wound up in the receiving line, Jonas and Bo could relax and enjoy meeting all their favorite pros and coaches. They offer a good example of a light approach to life.

And it made a great story the following week on their real job.

Use Humor to Open Hearts and Minds

In our presentation skills workshops, a frequent question our consultants receive is this: "When is it okay to use humor in a business or technical presentation?" Answer: Almost always. The follow-up question: "How do you define humor? And where do you position the humor so that it works best?"

Humor, whether in a presentation or a conversation, doesn't necessarily mean a joke or one-liner. In fact, jokes rarely work. If you've already heard them, assume that others have as well.

Having a sense of humor simply means the ability to see life in a lighthearted way. Those who see everything as a matter of life-and-death wear a permanent frown and make those around them ill at ease.

Personal anecdotes, humorous quotations or comments overheard on the street, a cartoon quip, a visual, a prop, a facial expression or gesture added at the appropriate moment—these are the humorous touches that work best after you've established rapport with your colleagues.

Simply your willingness and ability to "lighten up" can be invaluable in positioning yourself as a confident person, comfortable in unscripted situations.

Know What's Hot and What's Not

Your image can be tarnished irreparably when you use humor inappropriately. Several years ago, I spoke with a client about her needs for a new training program. She had asked our company to replace an instructor teaching their listening skills class. When I questioned her about the problem, she explained, "The course itself is fine. The instructor is the problem. She has absolutely no credibility with our group on the topic."

"Why is that?" I probed, curious as to how an instructor could not have credibility as a listener. It's not unusual that someone teaching leadership has not "led" any great organization, project, or effort. Or, a manager might be teaching negotiation skills without ever having negotiated a major contract. But no credibility as a *listener*? How could that be?

The client continued, "Well, the instructor would make a point about a good listening habit and even lead an exercise to practice it. But then she'd tell some funny incident about how she herself was a poor listener. For example, she emphasized the importance of listening carefully to people's names when introduced and presented a technique for remembering names. But then she told a story about going into the hospital ER last weekend with her mother, who had kidney stones, and made a joke about how she kept forgetting the nurses' names. She did that throughout the course—tell funny stories on herself as a poor listener until she had zero credibility with the class."

Humor helps break down walls, for sure. But presence demands at least a walkway of reserve to protect your credibility.

In addition to inappropriate self-deprecating humor, be wary of humor directed at others.

Consider the brouhaha that arose over the Don Imus incident, when he was fired as host of the "Imus in the Morning" show on MSNBC for his off-the-cuff derogatory remarks about the Rutgers women's basketball team (comments he thought were humorous and the public found otherwise).

Humor should be an affirmation of your humanity, not the cause of your downfall.

Heed These 10 Humor Hints

While humor eases stress, heals relationships, and positions you as a confident person, above all, it calls for good judgment. Keep these guidelines in mind:

---

10 Humor Hints to Make Connection and Retain Credibility

1. Avoid offensive humor such as racial or gender slurs.

2. Never make someone else uncomfortable as the butt of your humorous comments.

3. Use self-deprecating humor to endear yourself to an audience. Self-jabs demonstrate humility and vulnerability.

4. Make your humorous foibles understandable and never something that would diminish your credibility in others' eyes.

5. Respond "in the moment" to what's happening around you. These ad-libs play well with the crowd because they make you seem real and present.

6. Place a funny story later (after 2–3 minutes) in a presentation rather than earlier to get a better response. Laughter is a gift. Audiences must decide if they like you before they give you the gift of response.

7. Stand to the left side of the group when you deliver laugh lines and you'll get a better response (as opposed to the right side, where you should deliver emotional stories and appeals). This advice comes from comedians who make their living with humor.[28]

8. Pay attention to the size of the crowd when trying out new humor. Large groups respond to humor better than small groups. People feel self-conscious laughing loudly when they're in a small group. A large crowd lends anonymity.

9. Have some planned "saver" lines for the unexpected mishaps that often occur in formal situations (technology glitches, loud noises, late starts, fire drills).

10. When no one laughs, keep a straight face and maintain your poise as if you intended the story or comment to be serious. Make your point and move on.

Let those around you enjoy your company without feeling that they must be on guard for offense—for themselves or others. Your presence and good humor will be a refreshing lift in an otherwise routine day.

. . . .

Humor should be an affirmation of your dignity, not the cause of your downfall.

. . . .

19

. . . .

Commit to What
You Communicate

. . . .

Integrity is what we do, what we say,
and what we say we do.
—DON GALER

In the movie *Mr. Mom*, after the husband loses his job and has difficulty finding another, the stay-at-home wife goes to work while he stays home to care for the kids. The husband's self-esteem plummets when the wife's new boss stops by their house one morning to pick her up for an early meeting. Quickly, Mr. Mom arms himself with a buzz saw and goggles, throws out his chest in macho fashion, and struts to the door to greet the boss, pretending to be home on vacation, completing a remodeling project.

Looking around the family room, the boss asks, "So are you going to rewire everything in here?"

"Yeah. I'm doing all the electrical."

"Putting in 220, are you?" the boss asks.

"220. 221. Whatever it takes."

Cover blown.

It takes just one inappropriate action or comment to uncover the counterfeit. And once credibility vanishes, regaining it becomes a monumental task. People want to see the real you—the integrity behind your face, the actions behind your promises.

In today's economic landscape, trust trumps price.

Recently, my company was in the process of relocating our offices and selling some of our office furniture. The project manager from the firm handling our move invited three firms to bid on the project. While we were waiting on them to show up to tour the facility in order to prepare bids, he made this statement: "There are hundreds of firms out there. But I invited these three companies because I can count on them to show up and do what they say. And that's the name of the game these days. They may not give you the best bid, but they get it done. Companies will bid, and then just not do what they say. It's astounding to me. When you're relocating somebody and you have to have employees out of a building and into someplace else by a definite date, you need dependability."

He's talking about trust. Woody Allen got it right when he said, "Eighty percent of success is showing up." People with presence show up. They meet their commitments. That's another critical secret of their impact.

Yet some companies treat trust lightly every day. They put employees in positions where they're forced to lie and deceive. Ever responded to a promotional ad for a discount and walked into the store to discover they've "just sold out" but have another, slightly higher-priced model available? Ever consider switching phone companies for a period so you can come back later as a "new customer" and get their half-price rate? Ever sat on an airplane and wondered if the passenger beside you paid half as much or twice as much for the same ride? All such policies flout trust, and they drive loyal customers crazy.

Individuals create the same kind of resentment when they communicate things they don't mean, fail to keep confidences, and break commitments.

Practice the Principles You Preach

Consider your personal values for a moment rather than just work commitments. Let those around you know where you stand. If you believe in fiscal discipline, say so. If you think more money should be spent in research and development at the expense of granting raises or increasing the marketing budget, say so. If you think moving jobs overseas makes no sense, say so. If you think the organization needs to be more community-focused, let your views and values be known.

Whether others agree or not should be irrelevant. People respect those who speak their mind clearly and confidently—without carping when others disagree or decide not to go along.

But consistency counts. Even if others don't agree with your views, they expect to see consistency between what you say and what you do.

If you say you're devoted to your family, they don't expect you to be the office flirt. If you're serving on the United Way committee, they expect you to be a generous donor yourself. If you're hammering your staff to cut expenses, they don't want to discover that you're planning a four-day executive retreat in the Bahamas.

Ask Eliot Spitzer, New York governor and former Attorney General, who was known as "Mr. Clean" and was so outspoken about ethics and wrongdoing on Wall Street. He had prosecuted two prostitution rings before admitting to his own involvement in a prostitution ring known as the Emperor's Club VIP, despite having a wife and three children. Ask former North Carolina governor Mark Sanford, who preached family values, and then pleaded for forgiveness from the electorate when they discovered his affair with his Argentinian mistress. Ask Mel Gibson, actor and producer, about reaction to his racial outbursts when he's drunk and angry. Ask John Edwards how polls turned against him when knowledge of his affair with Rielle Hunter became public. Ask Anthony Weiner about the loyalty of colleagues after his photos surfaced.

Perception of someone's presence changes when there's a conflict between their personal and public values. Those once held in high regard find themselves laughingstocks.

The case for consistency even creates difficulty for fans in separating actors and actresses from the roles they play in their movies or TV series.

People want to see others live the roles, values, and standards

....

Life generally works well to the degree we do what we say.

....

they've created for themselves. Life generally works well to the degree we do what we say.

Tell the Truth

Embellishment happens as part of human nature. Ever since cave dwellers have been carving images on stones about the one that got away, people have been putting their best foot forward and that foot slips every now and then. The trouble now is that untruth may be sent out to the world via Twitter and live forever in cyberspace. Listeners may Google you fifty years from now and discover the deception.

In 2003, a study by the Society of Human Resources Management found that 53 percent of all job applications contain some kind of inaccurate information. In a 2008 CareerBuilder survey, only 8 percent of the respondents admitted to lying on their resumés, but almost half of the prospective employers said they had caught the applicant lying about some aspect of his or her qualifications. Result? Roughly 60 percent of these employers said they automatically dismissed applicants caught making misstatements.[29]

Telling the truth doesn't mean revealing everything you know. Some things should remain confidential. Some things are irrelevant to a discussion. You may not be able to reveal something for legal reasons or because doing so would violate the rights or privacy of others. When that's the case, either say so or remain silent on the subject. When you don't know something, it's perfectly acceptable to say you don't know and to tell someone you'll provide information when you have it or when you're free to do so.

But telling the truth means there's no place for lies or deception. In our Booher survey, we asked respondents to list the trait they considered the most important in a leader. Integrity/honesty received the highest response at 33 percent, with "authenticity/genuineness" a close second. If you don't have those two characteristics, nothing else matters much.

Similar results turned up in a 2010 study by Robert Half Management Resources. The firm interviewed more than 1,400 chief financial officers at randomly selected U.S. companies with 20 or more employees, asking them to identify the most important trait in prospective business leaders. To the question "Other than technical or functional expertise, which one of the following traits do you look for most when grooming future leaders at your organization?" "integrity" was cited by 33 percent. "Interpersonal/communication skills" was cited by 28 percent.[30]

> Without truth and authenticity, the essence of your presence has little foundation.

Without truth and authenticity, the essence of your presence has little foundation.

Follow Through

Having started my own business at age thirty, I've hired, fired, and contracted for services and goods from all sorts of suppliers, negotiated consulting and training services with Fortune 500 clients, coached executives, and worked with and observed professionals across myriad industries. Still I continue to be amazed at lack of follow-up in the marketplace. In my mind, that one facet of integrity has always separated the players from the batboys.

Follow-up means that you do what you say you'll do:

- If you say you'll put the check in the mail, you put the check in the mail.
- If you say you'll show up for the meeting, you show up for the meeting.
- If you say you'll finish the paperwork, you finish the paperwork.
- If you say you're going to cooperate, you cooperate.
- If you say you're going to keep something confidential, you keep the information private.
- If you say you're going to make improvements, you take the steps to do so.
- If you say you're going to deliver the product or service by X date, you deliver the product or service by X date.

Follow-up represents self-discipline—another perspective on the prism of personal presence. People with presence have impact on others because their words carry weight.

20

Show Up, Own Up, and
Straighten It Up

Men are alike in their promises.
It is only in their deeds that they differ.
—MOLIERE

Show me the money," from the movie *Jerry Maguire*, became a popular motto for good reason. People follow leaders who deliver results. The first public reaction to the announcement from the Obama administration that they had been "in charge of the BP oil spill from day one" was, "So show us the actions taken."

That's always the case and the question.

BP, Halliburton, Schlumberger all heard the same refrain from the public when they claimed things were "under control" after the largest oil spill in U.S. history: "So show me the action."

Likewise in any situation, whether routine or crisis, incompetence, refusal to accept responsibility for results, or whining diminishes the perception of personal presence.

Public reaction as registered by polls proved to be much more positive as President Obama spoke after the tragic Tucson shootings of Congresswoman Gabrielle Giffords and nineteen other victims by deranged gunman Jared Loughner. The president received praise as he spoke at a memorial service, encouraging the country to work together to create the kind of nation Christina Green, the nine-year-old victim of the shooter, imagined.

• • • • • • • • • • • • • • • • •

In any routine or crisis situation, incompetence, refusal to accept responsibility for results, or whining diminishes the perception of personal presence.

• • • • • • • • • • • • • • • • •

• • • • • • • • • • • • • • • • •

Everyone makes mistakes. It's how you recover that marks the winners and losers in life. . . . Apologies build, rather than destroy, credibility.

• • • • • • • • • • • • • • • • •

What marked the differences in the nation's responses to these two tragedies—the oil spill and the Tucson shooting—where many lives were lost and leaders of all political persuasions participated in the aftermath?

Admit Mistakes

Everyone makes mistakes. It's how you recover that marks the winners and losers in life. Expecting perfection in yourself or others sets an unattainable standard. Sooner or later, you're going to miss a beat. Apologies build, rather than destroy, credibility. Ask those who have done consumer research for years, and they will tell you the statistics on what they call "service recovery." When an organization makes a blunder with a customer and then offers an apology and makes it right, the vast majority of those customers become even more loyal than before the mistake.

Taking responsibility for wrong attitudes, for mistakes, or for inaction increases, rather than decreases, trust. In short, show up, own up, and straighten it up.

Be Accountable for Results

If you've ever "read between the lines" of a resumé, you understand the huge difference in being "accountable for" something and "responsible for" something. In resumé writing, it seems that if you're "responsible for" something, you've been assigned something. But in the real world, if you're accountable for something, someone is holding you accountable for an outcome, with the power to reward or penalize you, depending on that result.

Some resumés read like a job description: "Responsible for business development in a six-state region" or "Responsible for maintaining policy manuals with current updates." Interviewers always want to ask, "Well, how did you do? How much business did you develop in that six-state region you were responsible for? How well did you maintain those policy manuals? Did they get updated daily? Weekly? Quarterly? With what accuracy?" Resumés that report results make the top of the pile every time.

To repeat: Accountability implies risk and reward. You earn rewards for success; you accept penalties for failure. By the very nature of the risk-reward proposition, others' perception of your position and value increases.

Competence and results involve more than mere intelligence, per se. You probably know intelligent people who flunked out of school, who do poor work, or who can't get along with their peers. Likewise, you may know people of average intelligence who apply themselves to the job, do exceptional work, and motivate people to cooperate with them to achieve exceptional goals.

You've heard it said that money is not the most important thing in life. But that's easier to believe when you have enough of it to cover your basic needs. Likewise, people measure competence in different ways, and "enough" competence or "enough" intelligence becomes a matter of degree. At some point, people pull you over the "enough" threshold and begin to judge your performance on results.

Delivering the goods attracts attention and demands respect that translates into others' perception of your personal presence.

Track Progress and Make It Visible

Often you hear people say, "I just do a good job, and keep my head down." That philosophy works fine for avoiding controversy, but it restricts others' perception of your competence and contributions. If you expect people to take notice of your work, make it easy. Track it. Report it. No need to be obnoxious about it, but when asked, have data.

Never Whine

Constant complaining characterizes losers. The habit follows those who lack success and feel powerless to improve things for themselves. By their very act of whining, people are admitting that they lack the competence, character, communication skills, or commitment to improve things. Not a good message to send.

Second stringers sit on the bench, yell, and wag their head at the starters when they make mistakes. Winners take the field, accept the challenge, and take home the trophies.

A Final Note

Personal presence involves more than mojo and managing first impressions. Your presence involves your physical, mental, and emotional essence, as well as character. It encompasses what others think or feel about you, based on their interactions with you over time. When that feeling turns out to be favorable, you earn trust and credibility. As others experience the same thing in their interactions with you, buzz builds and social and business opportunities lead to personal and career success.

That impression of your presence rests on four key elements (see the chart on the following page).

The first step in increasing your personal presence is awareness. Observe people with presence: How do they look (move, gesture, walk, stand, dress)? How do they talk (word choices, intonation, conversational starters and bridges, emotional displays and control)? How do they think and communicate their thoughts in meetings, presentations, and writing? Finally, how do they demonstrate their character (integrity, concern, authenticity, goodwill, thoughtfulness, good humor, discipline, commitment)?

PERSONAL PRESENCE

LOOK
- Physical appearance, including body language, dress, accessories, grooming
- Energy, passion, spirit
- Surroundings such as personal work space

TALK
- Speaking patterns and vocal quality
- Tone of voice that reveals attitude
- Word choices and use of language
- Ability to carry on a conversation
- Emotional reactions and outbursts

THINK
- Capacity to think strategically, to cut through the clutter, to summarize well
- Ability to organize ideas coherently
- Ability to think visually and communicate with stories, analogies, metaphors, and sound bites to make messages clear and memorable
- Ability to think on your feet under pressure

ACT
- Acting consistently with integrity
- Demonstrating a willingness to listen to others' ideas
- Engaging with others; being approachable
- Being genuine
- Demonstrating thoughtfulness and good manners out of a sense of humility rather than arrogance
- Having a sense of humor
- Being competent and accountable for results

Your character serves as the foundation of the funnel. But your appearance is typically what others observe first about you. As you develop your presence in all four areas, you will increase your impact.

The second step involves personal assessment and feedback. Ask a trusted friend, supervisor, or peer for feedback on areas that concern you. Take the self-assessment product at www. bkconnection.com/personalpresence-sa to analyze yourself in the four key areas covered in the book.

The third step requires attention to habit and attitude and your commitment to learn and practice a new skill or technique. As you practice a new skill (such as larger gestures, thinking on your feet under pressure, or summarizing succinctly), ask your trusted coach for feedback. And make sure they've read the book and know what you're working to improve.

For an annual checkup, I suggest a video review. Dieters become discouraged when they lose only a pound or two a week and nobody seems to notice. But let them compare photos from January 1 and May 1 after they've lost twenty-five pounds, and they'll notice a dramatic difference! As with weight gain or loss, small increases in your personal presence may go unnoticed and seem insignificant to you week to week. But over time, you and others will see, hear, and feel the impact. As a baseline, record yourself in several situations (giving a presentation, leading a meeting, participating in a group discussion) and then record your first feedback from your trusted coach. A year later, record yourself in similar situations and compare the feedback sessions.

If you've been working at changes, you'll see and hear a significant increase in your personal presence and influence.

The good news about time and attention to this effort? With every interaction, you have the power to strengthen and communicate your presence. And as noted earlier whether you're starting a relationship, coaching a sports team, landing a job, closing a deal, or leading an organization through change, the little things can make a big impact.

The Personal Presence Self-Assessment

You may be interested in the Personal Presence Self-Assessment companion product referenced throughout the book. This twenty-seven-item online self-assessment is available at

www.bkconnection.com/personalpresence-sa

The assessment will help you measure your impact from low to high in all four areas discussed in the book: how you look, how you talk, how you think, and how you act. Your graphical results will also include an interpretation and tips. You may print out your customized Personal Presence profile and retake the self-assessment up to four times within a twelve-month period.

Bulk-order discounts are also available
for organizational programs.

Notes

1. Pease and Pease, *The Definitive Book of Body Language.*
2. Elmer and Houran, "Physical Attractiveness in the Workplace."
3. Case and Paxson, "Stature and Status," 499–532. See also Mobius and Rosenblat, "Why Beauty Matters," 222–235.
4. Cohen, *The Tall Book.*
5. Cialdini, *Influence,* 171.
6. Mobius and Rosenblat, "Why Beauty Matters," 222–235.
7. Pease and Pease, *The Definitive Book of Body Language.* They refer to this as the "Funnel Effect."
8. Robinson, TED Conference 2006.
9. For a complete list of image sources, see Photo Credits following About the Author.
10. Ekman, *Emotions Revealed.*
11. Pease and Pease, *The Definitive Book of Body Language,* 215–222.
12. Pease and Pease, *The Definitive Book of Body Language,* 71–72.
13. Freedman, "Why Trial Lawyers Say It Better."
14. Ekman, *Emotions Revealed,* 20–29.
15. Howard and Gengler, "Emotional Contagion Effects on Product Attitudes."
16. Ekman, *Emotions Revealed,* 58–60.
17. Tavris, *Anger: The Misunderstood Emotion.*
18. Bush, *Decision Points.*
19. Kanter, "Zoom In, Zoom Out," 112–116.
20. Burrus, *Flash Foresight.*
21. Cote, "A Balancing Act."
22. Jobs, "Commencement address at Stanford University."
23. Berman and Knight, *Financial Intelligence for Entrepreneurs,* 47.
24. Jones et al., "How Do I Love Thee? Let Me Count The Js," 665–683.

25. Cuddy, "Just Because I'm Nice, Don't Assume I'm Dumb."
26. Ickes, ed., *Empathic Accuracy*, 2.
27. Cialdini, *Influence*, 188–193.
28. Pease and Pease, *The Definitive Book of Body Language*, 340.
29. Knowledge@Wharton, "When Do Exaggerations and Misstatements Cross the Line?"
30. Gamble, "CFOs Cite Integrity As Most Important Trait," 18.

Bibliography

Ambady, Nalini, and Robert Rosenthal. "Half a Minute: Predicting Teacher Evaluations From Thin Slices of Nonverbal Behavior and Physical Attractiveness." *Journal of Personality and Social Psychology* 64.3 (1993): 431–441.

Axtell, Roger E., ed. *Do's and Taboos Around the World.* Third Ed. White Plains: The Parker Pen Company, 1993.

Baldoni, John. *Great Communication Secrets of Great Leaders.* New York: McGraw-Hill, 2003.

Berman, Karen, and Joe Knight with John Case. *Financial Intelligence for Entrepreneurs: What You Really Need to Know About the Numbers.* Boston: Harvard Business Press, 2008.

Booher, Dianna. *Communicate with Confidence: How to Say It Right the First Time and Every Time.* Rev. Ed. New York: McGraw-Hill, 2011.

———. *Speak with Confidence: Powerful Presentations That Inform, Inspire, and Persuade.* New York: McGraw-Hill, 2003.

———. *The Voice of Authority: 10 Communication Strategies Every Leader Needs to Know.* New York: McGraw-Hill, 2007.

Bowden, Mark. *Winning Body Language: Control the Conversation, Command Attention, and Convey the Right Message Without Saying a Word.* New York: McGraw-Hill, 2010.

Burg, Bob. "Act Your Way Into Really, Really Liking Them: Tips on Dealing with Difficult People." *SUCCESS Magazine*, December 2010: 19–21.

Burrus, Daniel. *Flash Foresight: How to See the Invisible and Do the Impossible.* New York: Harper Business, 2011.

Bush, George W. *Decision Points.* New York: Crown Publishing, 2010.

Carnegie, Dale. *How to Win Friends and Influence People.* New York: Simon and Schuster, 1936.

Case, Anne, and Christina Paxson. "Stature and Status: Height, Ability, and Labor Market Outcomes." *Journal of Political Economy* 116.3 (2008): 499–532.

Chaiken, Shelly. "Communicator Physical Attractiveness and Persuasion." *Journal of Personality and Social Psychology* 37.8 (1979): 1387–1397.

Cialdini, Robert B., Ph.D. *Influence: The Psychology of Persuasion.* Rev. Ed. New York: HarperCollins/Collins Business, 2006.

Cohen, Arianne. *The Tall Book.* New York: Bloomsbury, 2009.

Cote, Dave. "A Balancing Act: Federal Debt, Deficit, and Economic Recovery." Speech at the U.S. Chamber of Commerce, October 20, 2010. http://www51.honeywell.com/honeywell/common/documents/ceo -speeches-documents/Chamber_of_Commerce_Speech_-_10-19 _Final.pdf.

Cuddy, Amy J.C. "Just Because I'm Nice, Don't Assume I'm Dumb." *Harvard Business Review*, February 2009.

Dilenschneider, Robert L. *A Briefing for Leaders: Communication as the Ultimate Exercise of Power.* New York: Harper Business, 1992.

Dimitrius, Jo-Ellan, and Mark Mazzarella. *Reading People: How to Understand People and Predict Their Behavior Anytime, Anyplace.* New York: Random House, 1998.

Ekman, Paul. *Emotions Revealed: Recognizing Faces and Feelings to Improve Communication and Emotional Life.* New York: St. Martin's Press, 2003.

Elmer, Eddy, and Jim Houran. "Physical Attractiveness in the Workplace." 2008, Hotel News Resource, http://www.hotelnewsresource .com/article31439.html.

Freedman, Adam. "Why Trial Lawyers Say It Better." *The Wall Street Journal*, 29–30 January 2011.

Fugere, Brian, Chelsea Hardaway, and Jon Warshawsky. *Why Business People Speak Like Idiots: A Bullfighter's Guide.* New York: Simon & Schuster/Free Press, 2005.

Gamble, Cheryl. "CFOs Cite Integrity As Most Important Trait." *T+D*, December 2010.

Gladwell, Malcolm. *Blink: The Power of Thinking Without Thinking.* New York: Little, Brown and Company, 2005.

Goldsmith, Marshall. *What Got You Here Won't Get You There: How Successful People Become Even More Successful.* New York: Hyperion, 2007.

Goleman, Daniel. *Social Intelligence: The New Science of Human Relationships.* New York: Bantam Books, 2006.

Harvard Business School Press and the Society for Human Resource Management. *The Essentials of Power, Influence, and Persuasion.* Boston: Harvard Business School Press, 2006.

Helweg-Larsen, M. "To Nod or Not to Nod: An Observational Study of Nonverbal Communication and Status in Female and Male College Students." *Psychology of Women Quarterly* 28.4 (2004): 358–361.

Hess, Ursula, Reginald B. Adams, Jr., and Robert E. Kleck. "Who May Frown and Who Should Smile? Dominance, Affiliation, and the Display of Happiness and Anger." *Cognition and Emotion* 19.4 (2005): 515–536.

Howard, Daniel J., and Charles Gengler. "Emotional Contagion Effects on Product Attitudes." *Journal of Consumer Research* 28 (2001): 189–201.

Ickes, William, ed. *Empathic Accuracy.* New York: Guilford Press, 1997.

Jobs, Steve. "Commencement Address at Stanford University." Palo Alto, 12 June 2005.

Jones, John T., Brett W. Pelham, Mauricio Carvallo, and Matthew C. Mirenberg. "How Do I Love Thee? Let Me Count the Js: Implicit Egotism and Interpersonal Attraction." *Journal of Personality and Social Psychology* 87.5 (2004): 665–683.

Kanter, Rosabeth Moss. "Zoom In, Zoom Out." *Harvard Business Review*, March 2011.

Knowledge@Wharton. "When Do Exaggerations and Misstatements Cross the Line?" http://knowledge.wharton.upenn.edu. 23 June 2010. <http://knowledge.wharton.upenn.edu/article.cfm?articleid=2522>.

Kouzes, James M., and Barry Z. Posner. *Credibility: How Leaders Gain and Lose It, Why People Demand It.* San Francisco: John Wiley & Sons/Jossey-Bass, 2003.

Lizza, Ryan. "The Gatekeeper: Rahm Emmanuel on the Job." *The New Yorker*, 2 March 2009.

Lovas, Michael, and Pam Holloway. *Axis of Influence: How Credibility and Likeability Intersect to Drive Success.* New York: Morgan James, 2009.

Luntz, Frank. *Words That Work: It's Not What You Say, It's What People Hear.* New York: Hyperion, 2007.

Mehrabian, Albert, and Susan R. Ferris. "Inference of Attitudes from Nonverbal Communication in Two Channels." *Journal of Consulting Psychology* 31.3 (1967): 248–252.

Merhrabian, Albert, and Morton Wiener. "Decoding of Inconsistent Communications." *Journal of Personality and Social Psychology* 6.1 (1967): 109–114.

Mobius, Markus M., and Tanya S. Rosenblat. "Why Beauty Matters." *American Economic Review* 96.1 (2006): 222–235.

Nierenberg, Gerard I., and Henry H. Calero. *How to Read a Person Like a Book.* New York: Simon & Schuster/Pocket Books, 1971.

Noonan, Peggy. *Simply Speaking: How to Communicate Your Ideas with Style, Substance, and Clarity.* New York: Regan Books, 1998.

Pease, Allan, and Barbara Pease. *The Definitive Book of Body Language: The Hidden Meaning Behind People's Gestures and Expressions.* New York: Random House/Bantam Dell, 2004.

Pfeffer, Jeffrey. *Power: Why Some People Have It And Others Don't.* New York: HarperCollins/Harper Business, 2010.

Reiman, Tonya. *The Yes Factor: Get What You Want. Say What You Mean. The Secrets of Persuasive Communication.* New York: Penguin Group/Hudson Street Press, 2010.

Robinson, Sir Ken. TED Conference 2006. February 2006. Posted June 2006.

Shriver, Maria. *Just Who Will You Be?* New York: Hyperion, 2008.

Tavris, Carol. *Anger: The Misunderstood Emotion.* Rev. Ed. New York: Simon & Schuster/Touchstone, 1989.

Watson, Bruce. *PR Lessons from the Top: Tony Howard's Biggest Gaffes.* 22 June 2010. <http://www.dailyfinance.com/story/media/pr-lessons -tony-haywards-biggest-gaffes/19526309/>.

Willis, Janine and Alexander Todorov. "First Impressions: Making Up Your Mind After a 100-Ms Exposure to a Face." *Psychological Science* 17.7 (2006): 592–598.

Index

Photo Credits

Some of the photos used in Chapters 4 and 5 were purchased on a royalty-free license from www.dreamstime.com, as listed below. Figures 1, 2, 6, 7, 8, 11, and 22 are used courtesy of Jennifer Booher.

Figure 3. ©Andreg Skribans
Figure 4. ©David Gilder
Figures 5, 20, and 24. ©Yuri Arcurs
Figures 9 and 25. ©Andres Rodriguez
Figures 10 and 16. ©Elwynn
Figure 12. ©Andrzej Podsiad
Figure 13. ©Sophieso
Figure 14. ©Snezhok
Figure 15. ©Denis Pepin
Figure 17. ©Serdar Tibet
Figure 18. ©Olga Vasilkova
Figure 19. ©Kati1313
Figure 21. ©Geotrac
Figure 23. ©Olga Ekaterincheva

About the Author

Dianna Booher's life work has centered around communication in all its forms: oral, written, interpersonal, and organizational. As the author of forty-five books published in twenty-three countries and sixteen languages, she has traveled the globe talking with clients and organizations on six continents about the communication challenges they face at work and at home. Despite the cultural differences, two things remain the same: Communication is the basic business act. And communication either cements or destroys personal and work relationships.

To improve communication skills, habits, and attitudes dramatically changes life—for an individual, a family, an organization, and a nation. Dianna considers that an exciting and rewarding goal for her communication training firm, Booher Consultants.

Based in the Dallas/Fort Worth Metroplex, the firm provides communication coaching, training, and consulting to many of the Fortune 500 companies and governmental agencies, including IBM, Lockheed Martin, Raytheon, BP, Chevron, Ericcson, Alcatel-Lucent, USAA, Northwestern Mutual, Principal Financial, JPMorgan Chase, PepsiCo, Bayer, JCPenney, the Internal Revenue Service, Army and Air Force Exchange Service, U.S. Department of Veterans Affairs, and the U.S. Navy.

As one who likes to practice what she preaches about personal presence on the stage, Dianna stays busy on the speaking circuit. *Successful Meetings* magazine has named her to its list of "21 Top Speakers for the 21st Century." The National Speakers Association has awarded her its highest honor, induction into the Speakers Hall of Fame. *Executive Excellence* has named her to its list of *"100 Top Thought Leaders in America"* and *"100 Top Minds in Personal Development."*

Dianna's opinions on critical communication issues are frequently sought by the national media, including *Good Morning America, USA Today, Fox, CNN, CNBC, Bloomberg, Fortune, Forbes, The Wall Street Journal, Investor's Business Daily, NPR, The New York Times,* and *The Washington Post.*

She holds a master's degree from the University of Houston.

Contact Dianna and her team at www.booher.com or call 800.342.6621.

Resources by Dianna Booher
Available from Booher Consultants

Business Books

Booher's Rules of Business Grammar: 101 Fast and Easy Ways
    to Correct the Most Common Errors
Clean Up Your Act: Effective Ways to Organize Paperwork
    and Get It Out of Your Life
Communicate with Confidence®: How to Say It Right
    the First Time and Every Time, Revised Edition
The Complete Letterwriter's Almanac
E Writing: 21st Century Tools for Effective Communication
Executive's Portfolio of Model Speeches for All Occasions
From Contact to Contract: 496 Proven Sales Tips to Generate More Leads,
    Close More Deals, Exceed Your Goals, and Make More Money
Get a Life without Sacrificing Your Career
Get Ahead, Stay Ahead
Good Grief, Good Grammar
Great Personal Letters for Busy People
Speak with Confidence: Powerful Presentations
    That Inform, Inspire, and Persuade
The Voice of Authority: 10 Communication Strategies
    Every Leader Needs to Know
To the Letter: A Handbook of Model Letters for the Busy Executive
Winning Sales Letters

Inspirational Books

The Esther Effect
First Thing Monday Morning
Fresh-Cut Flowers for a Friend
The Little Book of Big Questions: Answers to Life's
    Perplexing Questions

Love Notes: From My Heart to Yours
Mother's Gifts to Me
Ten Smart Moves for Women
Well Connected: Power Your Own Soul by Plugging into Others
The Worth of a Woman's Words
Your Signature Work®: Creating Excellence and
   Influencing Others at Work
Your Signature Life®: Pursuing God's Best Every Day

Multimedia Programs
Communicate with Confidence®: Quick Tips with Dianna Booher
Effective Editing
Effective Writing
Good Grief, Good Grammar
More Good Grief, Good Grammar
Ready, Set, NeGOtiate
Sales Sizzlers®
Selling Skills and Strategies: Create and Deliver Sales
   Presentations with Impact
Selling Skills and Strategies: Everyone Sells:
   Selling Skills for the Non-Salesperson
Selling Skills and Strategies: Manage Your
   Pipeline, Accounts, and Time
Selling Skills and Strategies: Negotiate
   So That Everyone Wins
Selling Skills and Strategies: Thinking on Your Feet:
   Handling 11 Difficult Question Types
Selling Skills and Strategies: Write Proposals That Win the Business
Selling Skills and Strategies: Write to Your Buyers:
   Email, Letters, Reports
www.apologylettersonline.com
www.referencelettersonline.com
www.salesandmarketinglettersonline.com
www.sympathylettersonline.com
www.thankyoulettersonline.com

Workshops

Communicate with Confidence®
Customer Service Communications
Developing Winning Proposals
Email Matters®
eService Communications
Good Grief, Good Grammar
Listening Until You Really Hear
Meetings: Leading and Participating Productively
Negotiating So That Everyone Wins
Presentations That Work®
Resolving Conflict Without Punching Someone Out
Strategic Writing ™
Technical Writing

For More Information

For more information, please contact:
    Booher Consultants, Inc.
    Phone: 817-318-6000
    mailroom@booher.com
    Primary: www.Booher.com
    eStore: www.BooherDirect.com
    Blog: www.Booher.com/BooherBanter
    Twitter: @diannabooher
    Facebook: DiannaBooher
    LinkedIn: DiannaBooher

Berrett–Koehler
Publishers

Berrett-Koehler is an independent publisher dedicated to an ambitious mission: *Creating a World That Works for All*.

We believe that to truly create a better world, action is needed at all levels—individual, organizational, and societal. At the individual level, our publications help people align their lives with their values and with their aspirations for a better world. At the organizational level, our publications promote progressive leadership and management practices, socially responsible approaches to business, and humane and effective organizations. At the societal level, our publications advance social and economic justice, shared prosperity, sustainability, and new solutions to national and global issues.

A major theme of our publications is "Opening Up New Space." Berrett-Koehler titles challenge conventional thinking, introduce new ideas, and foster positive change. Their common quest is changing the underlying beliefs, mindsets, institutions, and structures that keep generating the same cycles of problems, no matter who our leaders are or what improvement programs we adopt.

We strive to practice what we preach—to operate our publishing company in line with the ideas in our books. At the core of our approach is stewardship, which we define as a deep sense of responsibility to administer the company for the benefit of all of our "stakeholder" groups: authors, customers, employees, investors, service providers, and the communities and environment around us.

We are grateful to the thousands of readers, authors, and other friends of the company who consider themselves to be part of the "BK Community." We hope that you, too, will join us in our mission.

A BK Life Book

This book is part of our BK Life series. BK Life books change people's lives. They help individuals improve their lives in ways that are beneficial for the families, organizations, communities, nations, and world in which they live and work. To find out more, visit **www.bk-life.com**.

Berrett–Koehler
Publishers

A community dedicated to creating
a world that works for all

Visit Our Website: www.bkconnection.com

Read book excerpts, see author videos and Internet movies, read
our authors' blogs, join discussion groups, download book apps, find
out about the BK Affiliate Network, browse subject-area libraries of
books, get special discounts, and more!

Subscribe to Our Free E-Newsletter, the *BK Communiqué*

Be the first to hear about new publications, special discount offers,
exclusive articles, news about bestsellers, and more! Get on the list
for our free e-newsletter by going to **www.bkconnection.com**.

Get Quantity Discounts

Berrett-Koehler books are available at quantity discounts for orders
of ten or more copies. Please call us toll-free at (800) 929-2929 or
email us at bkp.orders@aidcvt.com.

Join the BK Community

BKcommunity.com is a virtual meeting place where people from
around the world can engage with kindred spirits to create a world
that works for all. BKcommunity.com members may create their own
profiles, blog, start and participate in forums and discussion groups,
post photos and videos, answer surveys, announce and register for
upcoming events, and chat with others online in real time. Please join
the conversation!